D1558140

Pastoral Care in the BLACK Church

Pastoral Care in the BLACK Church

Edward P. Wimberly

ABINGDON

Nashville

Pastoral Care in the Black Church

Copyright © 1979 by Abingdon

Library of Congress Cataloging in Publication Data

WIMBERLY, EDWARD P 1943-
Pastoral care in the black church.
Includes bibliographical references.
1.   Pastoral theology.   2.   Afro-Americans—
Religion.   I.   Title.
BV4011.W49   253   78-22011

ISBN 0-687-30289-7

MANUFACTURED BY THE PARTHENON PRESS AT
NASHVILLE, TENNESSEE, UNITED STATES OF AMERICA

To my wife, Anne,
whose genuine caring has been
an inspiration to me

CONTENTS

PREFACE

Since the emergence of the black revolution in the mid 1950s there has been a growing concern in the black community for developing a body of literature reflecting the black experience. Up to the present time, there has been much literature examining the black church experience; however, very little material dealing with the pastoral care perspective has appeared. There is a real need to begin to develop a body of literature highlighting the importance of pastoral care in the black church. This book is an attempt to explore the black church experience in America from the pastoral care perspective. It is hoped that this work will help fill the literary void that exists as a result of the neglect of the pastoral care perspective.

I was motivated to explore the subject of pastoral care in the black church as a result of my doctoral studies at Boston University School of Theology. As a student, I worked in the South End of Boston with the Solomon Carter Fuller Mental Health Center as a pastoral consultant. My job was to attempt to relate black clergy to the mental health center. While working with black pastors, I became aware of the difference between what I was learning in pastoral care at the seminary and what was being practiced by these black pastors. This discrepancy triggered my curiosity, and I sought to examine in greater detail the phenomenon of black pastoral care. This book is the result.

This book has been written with black and white people, lay and clergy, and seminary student and professor in mind. I hope herein to make more explicit to the black pastor, the black lay person, and the black seminary student and professor the way in which pastoral care has been practiced in the black church. In reference to the white lay person, seminary student, and seminary faculty member, I hope to present the valuable contribution that the black church has made to pastoral care.

The basic theme of the book is that pastoral care is very much a part of black church tradition, although its emphasis may be different from that which is practiced in mainline white Protestantism today. The categories of traditional pastoral care—guiding, sustaining, healing, and reconciling—will be used to develop the theme of the book. The argument is that sustaining and guiding have been major functions of black pastoral care; and historical, social, and economic factors are drawn upon to support the thesis.

To the end of developing the theme, the book is divided into two parts. The first part examines and illustrates the historical and social context of black pastoral care. The second part attempts to develop a model of pastoral care for the black church reflecting many of the traditional functions and roles of black pastoral care and the discoveries of modern behavioral science. While the first part develops the basic thesis of the book, the second part builds upon the basic thesis to the end of fashioning a model for pastoral care.

Many persons have been influential in bringing this book to its final form. Immense gratitude goes to my wife, Anne, whose moral and practical assistance enabled me to finish my Ph.D. dissertation and my Ph.D. degree. This book is the direct result of that dissertation, at Boston University, and my wife typed portions of the book and the dissertation. She edited both works entirely. Without her help, it would have been impossible for me to have completed either this work or my doctorate.

Thanks also go to my parents, whose vocations stimulated my interest in pastoral care. Both my parents have backgrounds in ministry, counseling, and education. Special thanks go to my father for helping to give focus to my study of the tradition of pastoral care in the black church.

Special thanks also go to the following persons for editorial comments and assistance: Drs. Homer Jernigan, Merle Jordan, Thomas J. Pugh, and James Shopshire; and to Mrs. Lenora C. Evans, Mrs. Jimmie Williams, and Mrs. Georgia B. Wilkes for typing portions of the manuscript.

Finally, Dr. Grant S. Shockley, President of the Inter-denominational Theological Center, and Dr. Charles B. Copher, Dean of Academic Affairs, provided the financial assistance needed to complete the revisions of the manuscript. Their support and assistance was very timely and encouraging.

Pastoral Care in the BLACK Church

§

PART I

I
PASTORAL CARE IN THE BLACK CHURCH

Pastoral care is a communal concept. It exists whenever persons minister to one another in the name of God. In this light, pastoral care is not a new concept but has its theological roots in the Judeo-Christian tradition.

Pastoral care in the black church has a history. Many persons may have the impression that pastoral care does not exist in the black church because very little has been written about it. They may feel that pastoral care is a white-church phenomenon because of the many contributions made by white church people to its development in this country. But, to the contrary, any ministry of the church that has as its end the tender, solicitous care of persons in crisis is pastoral care. Pastoral care exists when the hungry are fed, when the naked are clothed, when the sick are healed, when the prisoners are visited. Therefore, it can be concluded that pastoral care has always existed in the black church because the needs of persons are ministered to by others all the time.

Following the premise that pastoral care exists wherever persons minister to the needs of others, our task is to examine the nature of pastoral care in the black church. For this purpose, pastoral care is defined as the bringing to bear upon persons and families in crisis the total caring resources of the church. Although such roles and functions as worship, church administration, preaching, and teaching are not generally considered pastoral care, they become resources for pastoral care when their dominant concern is for the care of individual persons and their families in crisis situations.

There are four functions that have characterized the way pastoral care has been practiced in the history of the Christian ministry. These four functions—healing, sustaining, guiding, and reconciling—have been examined and described by William A. Clebsch and Charles R. Jaekle.[1] *Healing* consists of binding up the wounds; repairing damage that has been done as the result of disease, infection, or invasion; and restoring a condition that has been lost. *Sustaining* refers to helping persons courageously and creatively endure and transcend difficult situations while preventing or lessening the impact of the situation;

sustaining is offered when healing is not possible. *Guiding* seeks to help persons in trouble make confident choices between alternative courses of action that will help them solve the problems they are facing. *Reconciliation* seeks to reestablish broken relationships between a person and God on the one hand, and between a person and other persons on the other.

For our purposes, the emphasis and the descriptive definitions given by Clebsch and Jaekle have been slightly altered. For example, they emphasize the pastor's role in carrying out the four functions of pastoral care. Because this book defines pastoral care as the bringing to bear of the total ministry of the church upon persons and families in crisis, we shall herein explore the prominent role of the total caring resources of the black church, particularly in relation to sustaining. In this context, the sustaining function is a ministry of the whole congregation as well as of the pastor. Sustaining may therefore be defined as bringing to bear upon the person in crisis the total caring resources of the church in such a way that the person is enabled to transcend and endure circumstances that are not immediately alterable.

The second exception to the definitions provided by Clebsch and Jaekle concerns the guiding function of pastoral care. Guiding refers to helping a person make choices between alternative courses of action; but rather than focusing upon courses of action alone, we will also consider the person's choice of the appropriate skills for coping with a crisis. This change in focus reflects our understanding of crisis as obstacles persons face which they cannot overcome by their usual problem-solving skills. Therefore, guiding refers to helping persons in crisis to choose positive, healthy crisis-coping mechanisms.

Another consideration reflects the way sociocultural forces affecting the black church shaped the nature of sustaining and guiding in black pastoral care. Because of the cultural situation within the black community, the black pastor is a symbol reflecting the hopes and aspirations of black people for liberation from oppression in this life. Therefore, when the black pastor engages in the functions of sustaining and guiding, his or her symbolic significance is brought to bear upon the person and family in crisis. In this book, the symbolic role of the black pastor in sustaining and guiding will have a prominent position.

While four functions have characterized pastoral care historically, two functions have dominated pastoral care in the black church. Clebsch and Jaekle point out that all four functions of pastoral care are present in every period of history, but one function may dominate in a particular era because of historical conditions. This is not the general rule in the history of pastoral care in the black church. Guiding and sustaining have both been dominant functions at the same time in the history of pastoral care in the black church; there has been no dominance of one over the other. While sustaining and guiding dominated, reconciliation took a secondary position, and healing became very difficult because of the racial climate. Therefore, more attention will be given to the equal dominance of sustaining and guiding in black pastoral care.

The fact that social oppression existed did not mean that healing did not take place in the black church. Although the black person's personality was damaged by racism and oppression, wholeness did come for many through the experience of God's love toward them. When the caring resources were brought to bear upon persons suffering from low self-esteem and self-hatred, they experienced themselves as accepted and as "somebody" in the eyes of God and their black brothers and sisters. Healing did exist for some, but for others sustenance was all that could be accomplished. For many, the burden of oppression made the love of God which transformed the self a distant hope; for them, God's love as mediated through the resources of the church prevented and lessened the impact of oppression.

Some explanation needs to be given concerning how sustaining and guiding became prominent in black pastoral care. The racial climate in America, from slavery to the present, has made sustaining and guiding more prominent than healing and reconciling. Racism and oppression have produced wounds in the black community that can be healed only to the extent that healing takes place in the structure of the total society. Therefore, the black church has had to find means to sustain and guide black persons in the midst of oppression. In this effort, much attention has been focused upon reducing the impact of racism upon the black personality, but it has been difficult to restore the wholeness of the person caused by the impact of oppression. People need guidance and hope in the present while making the most of their situation; at the same time they look forward to a future time of ultimate healing.

Reconciliation among persons has had a place in black pastoral care just as healing has had a place. Its place has been to lessen the division among persons so that the caring resources within the caring community would not be disrupted. Public confession has been one of the chief means of reconciling broken relationships, and thus it has

21

helped to maintain the integrity of the caring community. Thus, by preserving the integrity of the caring community whose resources were needed for the task of sustaining, reconciliation has served the end of sustaining.

Reconciliation with God has also served the sustaining function of black pastoral care, being subsumed under sustaining because of the nature of social reality. Reconciliation, or union, with God is the ultimate goal of the black Christian, but it must be viewed in the context of the oppression and powerlessness of black people. Because of oppression, union with God has meant uniting with the source of the power of the universe for the purposes of being supported and sustained in life.[2] Reconciliation has had an end beyond mystical union with God or life after death for the black Christian. It has had implications for living, for being sustained in the presence of oppression.

Before concluding this section, there needs to be some indication of how black pastoral care differs from the modern pastoral-care movement in white mainline Protestant denominations. Owing to the historical circumstances of the black church, pastoral care has had a different focus than in mainline Protestant white churches. Healing has been the dominant function in these white denominations largely because of the absence of economic, political, and social oppression. The healing model of modern pastoral care goes back to the early 1920s, and it was predominantly influenced by the one-to-one Freudian psychoanalytic orientation to psychiatry.[3] To learn the methods and skills of the one-to-one healing model requires economic resources and extensive clinical and educational opportunities to which many black pastors did not have access until very recently. Therefore, healing could become a tradition in the mainline Protestant white churches because there were economic resources to provide clinical training for pastors, whereas the black church had to rely upon a tradition of sustaining and guiding fashioned in response to oppression.

The fact that the early roots of pastoral care in white Protestant denominations were largely nourished by the one-to-one model of medical psychiatry made such models difficult for the black pastor to appropriate in the local church. The black pastor needed an orientation that would help him or her utilize the resources within the black church in the care of souls. The creativity of many black pastors has been evidenced in their finding corporate and communal means to meet the needs of persons when theoretical models were inadequate.

In the remaining sections of this chapter, an examination of the historical roots of sustaining and guiding in the black church will be undertaken.

A SUSTAINING MINISTRY

Unlike the sustaining function in the healing tradition of mainstream Protestant pastoral care, sustaining in the black church tradition has not been the function of the pastor alone. The sustaining dimension of black pastoral care has been the function of the total church acting as the caring community. It was not just the pastor who looked after the spiritual and emotional needs of the church members; the whole caring community provided the sustenance for persons and families in crisis situations. As a caring community, the black church has drawn upon many significant resources to enable persons to overcome and endure the numerous crises arising in the normal course of life exacerbated by oppression. For example, the caring community supported many of the personality needs of its members. It provided supportive structures for persons as they passed through the normal stages of the life cycle. It developed an important theological worldview that enabled the black person to find hope to endure the mundane problems of living in a hostile world. These caring resources will be examined in greater detail in the next sections.

Slavery

Slavery marked the beginning of the black person's journey in America. The slaves were forcibly removed from their native soil and sold away from their families in America. Forced to work without pay, they were stripped of any power to determine their own existence. They were viewed as property and regarded as subhuman. It was against this background that many of the important resources for sustaining were developed.

In the nineteenth century the black church came into existence as an independent institution. Prior to this time, it existed as an invisible institution meeting in clandestine fashion.[4] Many community resources emerged from the invisible and visible institution for the support of persons. These resources included the family, the extended family, peers, the social network, the church fellowship, and the rituals and ceremonies of the visible and invisible church. Sustaining as a function of pastoral care emerged as a corporate function of the community.

A theological world view was one of the most important community resources for sustaining during slavery. A world view is a system of symbols that integrates and synthesizes experiences in order to provide the meaning of existence.[5] In the context of pastoral care, a world view undergirded the caring resources. In the case of the slave, a world view emerged that not only gave meaning to the slave's existence but also provided the efficacious power that sustained the slave in a hostile environment.

The world view of the slave projected God as the important resource of sustaining. For the slave, God was envisaged as being immanently involved in all of life, and he was the ultimate source of life. The world view provided explanations of how God had power over the universe, and held that faith in him provided the power to sustain the slave in the midst of chaos. The slaves believed God was in control of the matters of the world and in his own time would make things right in the world.

The Negro spirituals reflected much of the slaves' world view. Through the singing of the Negro spiritual, the slave was actually participating in the sustaining power of God. As shared creations emerging out of a common condition, many of the Negro spirituals provided a view of the world that enabled the slaves to transcend the brutality of everyday existence. Some provided a faith in a sustaining power that transformed the slaves' despair over the cruelties of slavery into hope. The spirituals helped the slave find meaning and purpose for existence. Through the world view expressed in the spiritual, the slave was provided with a deep capacity for endurance in spite of suffering. It was the faith expressed in many of the spirituals that sustained the slave through life.

The uniqueness of Negro spirituals lies in their reflection of the faith that undergirded the caring life of the black church. Their world view provided not only sustaining power for individual persons, but also the glue that held the caring community together. Many of the spirituals reflected a faith that God was intimately involved in the life of specific communities and that he had not exhausted all his resources for conquering evil. Some of the spirituals reflected an incarnational faith that God became the companion of persons within the community for the purposes of caring for a suffering humanity. This belief sustained the care that persons gave one another.

In addition to this world view, another community resource for sustaining during slavery was the ritual of baptism. Baptism, in most mainline white churches, would fall into the category of reconciliation; but, as we indicated earlier, in the black church, reconciliation was subsumed under sustaining for historical reasons.

One function of sustaining in the black church during slavery was to provide symbolic means for the slave to unite with the source of power and care in the universe. It was through the symbolic means of baptism that the slave sought to be put in touch with God. It was through *immersing* that the slave found symbolic unity with God and obtained the power for survival. It was through the power of God working through the caring community that persons being baptized found the power to live a new life in a strange world.

Not only was the ritual of baptism an important means of sustaining, but the black church as an extended family for the slave was also a tremendous resource. The black church provided surrogates to replace the slave's relatives who had been sold away. Within the church, children who had been sold away from their parents could find substitute parents and parental images. Moreover, the black church attempted to provide moral support for the restoration of the black male to black families. The black church tried to emphasize the Old Testament cultural ideal of the responsibility of the father in the Jewish family.[6] In addition, the church served as an agency of social control whose aim was to strengthen and stabilize the black family by emphasizing patterns that were healthy to family and community life.[7] The total ministry of the black church was thus concentrated on the attempt to heal the wounds in black families during slavery.

The black church also provided community resources to support persons during life crises. One crisis in the black community during slavery was death. Because the slaves were viewed as property that could be expendable, they lived in the constant shadow of death. Consequently, they sought to create social structures within the life of the community and the church to help them deal with death when it came.

During the eighteenth century, mutual-aid societies and burial societies emerge in the black church to provide economic and moral support systems for persons during bereavement. According to Frazier, the earliest mutual-aid society was the Free African Society organized in Philadelphia in 1787 by Absalom Jones and Richard Allen.[8] This society's purpose was to support its members in sickness and to benefit the surviving spouse and the children of the deceased. Financial aid as well as caring concern was offered. Another beneficial society was the Brown Fellowship Society in Charleston, South Carolina, which was designed to relieve widows and orphans during distress, sickness, and death.[9] These mutual-aid societies developed significantly during the emancipation of the slaves and continued to expand for many decades in black churches.

Through these societies, the community emphasis in pastoral care in the black church can be visualized.

Another important resource of the black church for sustaining was the therapeutic nature of black worship. Because of the holistic view of persons in black religion, people's feelings were not ignored or considered unimportant. In fact, the black church helped the slaves to realize that their feelings were essential to their very being, for it was through the slaves' feelings that they recognized what they valued most and what they aspired to in life. The slaves desired more than anything else their freedom and the right to determine the directions for their own lives. However, freedom and self-direction were denied, and, as a result, the slaves had to find an outlet for their frustrated feelings. The black church provided an avenue for the expression of their shattered dreams. Black worship served as a catharsis by which the slaves could release pent-up emotions. It served as an important avenue of expression for the whole personality.

The therapeutic value of black worship as a resource of pastoral care is pointed out by Melville Herskovits. "That repression is a cause of neurosis is an elementary tenet of psychoanalysis; the fact, explained in different terms, has been recognized by Negroes."[10] In worship, persons' feelings of frustration with the conditions of life were accepted as real. Such feelings were not ignored by others who shared the same situation in life; and through the acceptance of their feelings, individuals found they were loved and cared for by others. In the context of worship, persons' feelings of frustration were shared and accepted, and they administered pastoral care to one another.

In summary, the community resources for sustaining the

slave included symbols, rituals, and social groups. These resources helped sustain the slave in the face of injustice, but they could not heal the wounds from the injustice that was inflicted. It must be pointed out, however, that forces for liberation were operating in slavery through violent rebellions and the underground railroad. For the slave, healing meant liberation from oppression; therefore, it was impossible to repair the damage done by slavery without manumission.

Sustaining Between 1910 and 1950

The basic resources for sustaining during slavery existed also in the period from 1910 to 1950. The caring resources of the community continued to support persons during crisis situations. The same world view, which portrayed God as immanently involved in the life of the community, continued. However, many of the social conditions that existed during slavery changed in this period, and this meant that the community resources had to be applied to different circumstances.

Although slavery was abolished by the Emancipation Proclamation, racism continued into the twentieth century. White people's attitude toward black people continued to reflect the assumption of inferiority. More violence replaced the slave system as one of the mechanisms to reenslave the black person. Jim Crow laws were enacted to support segregation. By 1921, all the political, social, and economic gains made by black people during the Reconstruction period became null and void.

Against this backdrop of racism, violence, and disfranchisement, many Southern black people turned Northward to attempt to secure freedom. In 1900, the rural black population in the United States was 77 percent of the total black population. By 1910, the rural part of the black population had dropped to 72 per cent, and by 1920 to 66 percent. It is obvious that the rural population was changing.

Migration of the rural Southern black people to Northern urban areas took place during this period. Not only was freedom an attraction for rural Southern black people, but job opportunities also lured them to the city. Many jobs were created after the end of World War I and the influx of European immigrants halted. This migration of rural black people was also accelerated by the collapse of the cotton crop due to the boll weevil and the unusual floods in 1915. The end result was the Great Migration, which continued through the Depression and World War II unabated.

Naturally, the black church expanded into Northern cities as a result of the Great Migration. Many new black churches emerged during this period to meet the emotional needs of persons.

The migration to the urban North and the continuation of racism exacerbated the problems of black people. The black person's self-esteem was threatened because of negative feedback from the wider society. There was a crisis of powerlessness caused by exclusion from full participation in the wider society, and there were the problems associated with adjusting to the depersonalized city. The sustaining ministry emerged during this period to help the black person adjust to these new circumstances.

The black church became a community resource for sustaining the black person's self-esteem in the midst of powerlessness. In fact, the black church became an alternative structure which substituted for economic and political participation in the wider society. Many parishioners found sustenance for their self-esteem by being part of a successful institution that was able to support itself and provide economic support through small business ventures and credit unions. Moreover, people could exercise political awareness through participation in the decision-making processes of the local church. As an alternative structure, the black church did not heal the problems associated with exclusion from full participation in the wider society; however, it did prevent further damage to black self-esteem.

Perhaps the greatest sustaining ministry of the black church during this period was the care given to the uprooted Southern migrants that helped them adjust to the depersonalized urban environment. This care was manifested through the community support systems which the black church provided. Large, established churches in the urban North provided many types of supportive activities during this period.[11] These activities included scouting, recreation, youth programs, and camping. Some of these churches had community workers, day nurseries, community houses, and clinics. All these churches offered the migrants such traditional services as Sunday school, choir activities, and prayer meetings. Moreover, remnants of the old benevolent burial societies, which were developed during slavery, continued.

These resources provided a stabilizing influence for the uprooted Southern migrants by helping to support a sense of family unity among the migrants. Many left their families behind and sent for them later, after they found jobs. These people suffered feelings of being uprooted and isolated. The church's resources helped these black persons overcome feelings of isolation by helping them relate to others.

Moreover, the black church functioned as a port of entry for the migrants, helping them adjust to urban life. Many of the migrants had never been to the city; they were straight from the rural areas and farm economy. They needed help in finding housing and jobs. Since the black church was the gathering place for the whole black community, it served many of thé needs of persons by helping them find housing and jobs.

The black church also provided opportunities for persons to find emotional support for coping with urban ills. One such opportunity was the prayer meeting. The average attendance at prayer meetings during this period was thirty-nine.[12] These meetings, characterized by a warm interpersonal environment, were conducted in an atmosphere of freedom of expression. Extemporaneous prayers, songs, and personal testimonies contributed to the air of spontaneity and support. Biblical instruction was an undergirding influence in these sessions. In these surroundings, individuals found themselves cared for and accepted. This acceptance provided an important experience in the lives of those adjusting to an impersonal urban environment.

The storefront church performed a significant ministry of sustaining during this period. Many migrants suffered from cultural shock as a result of migration. The urban enviroment was much different from the rural environment: people lived on top of one another; there were no farms, only paved streets. It was impossible for the migrant to know everybody as he did in the rural areas. The drastic change in culture presented the migrant with an extremely difficult psychological adjustment. Many persons turned to the traditional established denominational church for a sense of community. However, once the migrants were settled, they became dissatisfied with these traditional denominations, because they were too different from the churches they had left in the rural South. Many migrants began to develop their own churches as a result, patterned after those which were most familiar to them, the rural churches. These churches were very small and usually met in small storefronts. Thus, the storefront phenomenon emerged in the city.

The basic function of the ministry of sustaining in these storefront churches was to help the migrant feel at home in the city. The migrant had difficulty adjusting to the impersonal urban environment. Therefore, the storefront church sought to gear its sustaining ministry to attempting to help the migrant feel comfortable in a strange new world.

These small storefront churches helped prevent a feeling of isolation through the social nature of the worship experience and through the opportunity for fellowship and personal recognition.[13] Within the storefront church, the migrants could sing the same songs they sang in the rural areas. They could be expressive in worship. They could gather with friends. The migrants found the storefront church very supportive in making their adjustment to urban living.

Sustaining Since 1960

Beginning in the mid 1950s, events in the United States laid the groundwork for the full participation of black people in American society. The civil rights movement, the black power movement, the involvement of Congress, the executive branch, and the Supreme Court introduced a new era of race relations in America.

The doors of full participation have been opened to many black people, although some of the old racist attitudes still prevail. Because of the entry of black people into the mainstream, some of the functions performed by the black church have been relinquished to secular agencies. The centralized role of the black church in the black community has been weakening; and the old supportive resources for sustaining black people, though still in existence, are disappearing. The task of ministry in the future is to revitalize many of the supportive structures of the black church and give them new meaning in the light of a changed condition. Many economic, social, and emotional problems still exist for black people, even though oppressive structures have been modified and secular agencies exist to respond to these needs. Therefore, a ministry that will sustain people in their pursuit of a meaningful life within American society is still relevant.

THE SYMBOLIC ROLE OF THE PASTOR

Sustaining and the Black Pastor

The discussion so far has emphasized the role of corporate caring resources in sustaining persons. There needs to be some explanation of the role the black pastor has performed in sustaining persons. This role has largely been that of a symbol—that is, he or she has been an articulator of the theological world view and a presider over the rituals and ceremonies that provided sustenance. The major function of the black pastor has been to be the leader of the corporate community in utilizing its resources; and when these resources were brought to bear upon the lives of persons in crisis, the symbolic role of the pastor became a function of pastoral care.

As a leader of the community, the black pastor has been the custodian of the community world view. From the pulpit he or she expounded the faith of the community that enabled persons to endure the hardships of life and proclaimed a faith in a God who was incarnate in life and whose purpose was tied to the lives of black people. The pastor made sure that the faith of the community was constantly before it so that the people found meaning for life. In presiding over baptism and communion, the pastor made the world view and its power to sustain available to the parishioner. The role of the pastor as leader was crucial, because without such leadership, the corporate resources for sustaining persons in crisis lost some of their meaning. More will be said about the symbolic role of the black pastor in the next section.

Guiding and the Black Pastor

The black community has given a significant place to the black minister historically, and the leadership role of the pastor has been significant in shaping the sustaining and guiding functions and making them the major emphasis in pastoral care in the black church.

Every living system possesses an identity. This identity is expressed in goals and values that are embodied in symbols. These symbols are standards of reference to which the people look to find meaning, purpose, and guidance. In this context the pastor, by virtue of his or her office, is the major symbol of the church, according to Mansell Pattison.[14] His or her function as a symbol provides a continuing affirmation of the community's identity, its goals, its values, and its purposes. Pattison comments on the importance of the symbolic significance of the minister: "The minister's very presence carries with it an implicit message. The pastor is a systemic reminder of what the system is."

The black pastor is and has been the symbol of the black church. The presence of a minister in the black community evokes many responses, both positive and negative. In either case the emotional response is strong, and no other person has been given a more centralized role in the black community.[15] The black pastor reminds the people of who they are—children of God living in a hostile environment. More than this, he or she symbolizes for some people God's engagement in the life of humankind, while for others he or she symbolizes God's absence or hiddenness from humankind. For many black people, however, the minister is a representative of God and therefore should be accorded respect.

Because of the symbolic nature of the role of the black minister, he or she has been accorded leadership authority of great magnitude. Many people in the black community have assigned to the black pastor wisdom and competence in all matters of living. He or she is expected to provide a worldview so that the parishioner can integrate his or her own experience. Because of this assignment, many of the laity have expected the minister to be omniscient, omnipotent, and omnipresent, and to provide solutions to many earthly problems as well as to be a custodian of the values connecting them to God. Although no human could live up to these expectations, they have been operative among the laity, and the pastor has tried to live up to them as much as possible.

Because of this leadership expectation by black people, the guiding function of pastoral care became dominant. The black pastor, namely the male, became the spiritual father and leader of the black people, and was expected to guide the congregation. He was expected to display no weakness at all, and he was expected to be in full charge and control of the church. In personal matters of pastoral concern, the pastor was expected to take charge and provide answers and solutions. Many people looked to the minister as a father in pastoral concerns, and this included elderly people. The prominence of the black pastor's authority came as a result of the fact that the church was the center of the community and that this church was full of persons whose earthly power had been frustrated.[16]

Recently, the central role of the pastor in leadership has changed in the black church. Since the 1950s, progress in race relations has opened new opportunities for black leadership in the wider society. Slowly, black people have begun to look away from the church for leadership, because more and more black people are being educated and trained. Opportunities for black lay people outside the church have been lessening the influence of the black preacher. As a result of this new development, many pastors are in the midst of an identity crisis and need help in developing new skills of guiding. In the future, the black laity will need guidance, but the guidance will have to take more cognizance of the parishioner's internal abilities. The pastor's guidance will be less authoritarian and more enabling of persons' own abilities and potential for making their own decisions.

SUMMARY

The sustaining and guiding functions of pastoral care have had equal prominence in black pastoral care. Unlike the alternating dominant-function hypothesis described by Clebsch and Jaekle, there have been two functions, not one, operating simultaneously in black pastoral care. This has been true because of socio-cultural circumstances. It was very difficult for the healing function to emerge because oppression made wounds almost irreparable, and reconciling became a function performed under sustaining.

Historically, sustaining has been the function of the total church in black pastoral care. In this context the pastor and the congregation have worked together to sustain persons in crisis. Not only have the congregation and the pastor represented significant resources for pastoral care, but other cultural religious resources have been drawn upon for the care of persons. Among these resources have been the religious world view, ritual practices, and the symbolic significance of the black pastor.

II
THE PARENTING FUNCTION:
THE CRISIS OF GROWING OLD

The black pastor has been expected, as a symbol of the community, to help the person in crisis find meaning for his or her existence. Often the expectation has been that the pastor would provide specific advice and direction to the person. In some instances, the pastor was expected to take over and to take charge. This taking-over function is called parenting. In the case study to follow, parenting as a means of bringing the sustaining resources of the church to bear upon an elderly woman in the crisis of senescence will be examined. The aim of this chapter is to illustrate how parenting can help lessen the negative impact of aging upon a person.

A CASE STUDY

Mrs. Smith was seen walking the streets of a large Northern city in an apparently disorganized state of mind. Many of the community members who knew Mrs. Smith attempted to relate to her, but she refused and rebuffed their help. Members of the neighborhood community center got involved also, and she refused their help. When all care-taking efforts had failed, Mrs. Smith's pastor was called.

After being informed of Mrs. Smith's condition, the pastor did not hesitate to begin his search for her. He drove down every street in the community surrounding Mrs. Smith's home. Finally he found her, very disorganized and emotionally spent. She was weak and very untidy.

The pastor described Mrs. Smith's general characteristics and her social history. Over a four-year period, he had come to know her very well. She was seventy-three years old and had worked as a domestic cleaning woman until her seventy-second birthday. She was not well-educated, but she could read and count. She served in the church as the financial secretary and was a regular churchgoer. Mrs. Smith had no living relatives in the North, and her husband had left her over thirty years earlier. She had never known her parents, and she was raised by relatives until she was old enough to go to work for rich white people.

The pastor said that after a short conversation with Mrs. Smith, she revealed the heart of her problem. Her crisis began when she could no longer work as a domestic and received her first Social Security check. Since there were no real records kept of her birth in the South, a friendly white employer had filed Social Security papers for Mrs. Smith many years earlier. The employer had used Mrs. Smith's own recollection of events in her life to derive an age for her. However, Mrs. Smith felt that the age reported for her was incorrect and that the Social Security agency would find out how old she really was and arrest her for fraud. The problem was that Mrs. Smith did not believe she was seventy-three years old.

When the pastor found her on the street, he took her home, but when he helped her into her house she became very frightened and refused to stay inside. She said the FBI men were in the house and had come to arrest her for fraud.

The minister feared for Mrs. Smith's well-being, so he took her home with him. During the night, the pastor and his wife were awakened by Mrs. Smith's talking. Mrs. Smith was calling to her deceased mother. The pastor and his wife remained up all night trying to listen to her and console her. The pastor said he felt very sad because Mrs. Smith reminded him of a little girl who had just lost her mother. According to the pastor, the only thing that calmed her down was his wife's holding Mrs. Smith in her arms while she cried.

The pastor and his wife found that Mrs. Smith needed constant care. She improved some, but she quickly became disoriented when left alone too long. Since the pastor and his wife had obligations outside their home, they consulted with one of the community caretakers for help. The caretaker suggested that Mrs. Smith have a psychiatric examination. The pastor finally consented after some initial resistance. The psychiatric examination revealed that Mrs. Smith was not emotionally ill but that she found it very hard to adjust to retirement in a world where her loved ones were missing. The psychiatrist gave Mrs. Smith some medication, and the pastor, who sat through the examination, took Mrs. Smith to her home.

When she arrived home, she was much calmer and was not fearful of staying in the house. The pastor visited her every day for about two weeks and encouraged her to keep taking her medication. She also had problems budgeting her small Social Security income. The pastor interceded with the old-age assistance department of the welfare office, so that she could receive additional assistance.

The pastor said he did not try to do everything himself. He encouraged the church members to call on her and take her places in the community. Moreover, he encouraged her to join groups for the elderly at the neighborhood center. He felt that Mrs. Smith needed to establish a substitute family in the church and in the community.

Slowly, Mrs. Smith began to feel better about life. Although she was not able to recapture the lost years and lost loved ones, she was able to make the most of her remaining years.

ANALYSIS OF THE PASTOR'S ROLE

In this section, I will examine, in some detail, the sustaining role of the black pastor.

Parenting as Sustaining

As indicated earlier, one of the real sources of the sustaining role of black pastors has been the expectation of black parishioners. Black pastors have been expected in cultural tradition to be the shepherds who care for the sheep in times of difficulty. This traditional expectation, moreover, had its origin in slavery where the homeless black person found a family in the church. In the case just presented, the pastor and his wife became the symbolic parents of the homeless woman. This parenting expectation is explained by Floyd Massey, Jr., and Samuel B. McKinney:

> The black lay person has considered the pastor a father, regardless of the leader's age. It is not unusual for an 80 year old church member to tell a young pastor, "You are the father of us all" and to the pastor's wife these words would be uttered: "You are our mother."
>
> The fatherly image of the pastor has been linked to that of a shepherd. The shepherd led, fed, protected, corrected, and supported the flock. For black people, the shepherd was the pastor; the flock was the congregation, and the sheepfold was the building.[1]

In the case of Mrs. Smith she expected the pastor and his wife to be surrogate parents. When Mrs. Smith's behavior is analyzed according to the unconscious-transference model of psychoanalysis, it is seen to reveal a clear abnormal expectation with origins in her own psychic condition rather than outside her in culturally learned patterns. Moreover, the psychoanalytic model would suggest that the black pastor was responding to his inner needs to be a father when he responded positively to the parishioner's expectation. However, the pastor sensed that Mrs. Smith's need was real, and he responded to her expectation according to the role taught by his culture. He and his wife became her temporary parents. However, the pastor was not trapped by his culturally learned role. He realized that he and his wife had limitations and could not follow through on the role totally. If he were to respond to Mrs. Smith totally out of his own needs, he would not be able to set limitations.

The willingness of her pastor to assume the temporary parenting role helped to sustain Mrs. Smith in her crisis. Surely, the willingness of the pastor and his wife to assume this role was a sustaining force in Mrs. Smith's life. She felt very secure in their home. There was also some improvement in her condition after the overnight stay. In reality, the pastor and his wife were able to give Mrs. Smith the kind of ego support that temporarily fulfilled her need to be parented.

Following the psychiatrist's drug treatment, Mrs. Smith's pastor continued the fathering role with some modifications. He visited every day, and took the leading role in seeing that she received old-age assistance. However, he began to wean her by encouraging others in the congregation to help her. Moreover, he suggested that she take an active role in establishing her own new family at the church and in the programs for the elderly. Therefore, the pastor viewed his role of parent as something necessary but temporary. When Mrs. Smith began to get her own ego strength back, he relinquished his parenting role.

The Black Pastor and Preservation

Preservation is that aspect of sustaining that holds the line against threats of loss and against emotional deterioration that could result from this loss.[2] Mrs. Smith's problem was associated with growing old, and her fear of a possible conflict with the Social Security department intensified the problem. Retiring brought on feelings of extreme loneliness, and she became aware of how difficult it was to live without loved ones. Pastoral intervention prevented Mrs. Smith from sinking further into despair and from losing hope in the possibility of finding meaning for her life while growing older. Indeed, if the line had not been held against despair, Mrs. Smith would probably have given up on life and died.

The pastor's getting the congregation involved also helped Mrs. Smith overcome despair. They became her surrogate family, sustaining her for many years following that crisis.

The Black Pastor and Consolation

Another aspect of sustaining is consolation. Consolation assists a person in regrouping his or her remaining personal resources in a crisis situation.[3] In Mrs. Smith's case, there were many personal resources that she could use in adjusting to a world without loved ones. Although her pastor functioned in an active parenting fashion, there were many areas of decision-making in which she had to perform. She had to take her medicine periodically during the day. She had to resume cooking and cleaning responsibilities for herself. She had to pay her bills and do her shopping. In other words, she had the resources to do a great deal for herself. In fact, her pastor relinquished his parenting role when she assumed more and more of her own responsibilities. This was demonstrated in his encouraging her to build her own substitute family.

The pastor's willingness to assume the parenting role prevented Mrs. Smith from being overwhelmed by despair. Conversely, the pastor's willingness to relinquish the parenting role enabled Mrs. Smith to gradually use more and more of her own resources to cope with her crisis.

The Black Pastor and Redemption

The final function of sustaining is redemption. Redemption takes place when a person begins to build a new life although there is no possibility of restoring the loss he or she has suffered.[4] As a result of the intervention by the pastor, his wife, and the congregation, Mrs. Smith was able to resume full participation in life. Although she would never regain her youth or her lost loved ones, she was able to find new meaning through her new surrogate family. She had overcome her loneliness with courage, and she was able to take advantage of some of the opportunities that came to her late in her life. She never stopped growing.

The Black Pastor and Problem Solving

In the case above, the pastor took a practical problem-solving approach to Mrs. Smith's crisis. Because of his long relationship with her over the years, he had some idea of the major events in her life. Moreover, he did enough data collection to find out that retirement and loss of employment had provided the impetus for the problem.

The immediate problem for the pastor was to help Mrs. Smith regain a sense of reality. He did this by assuming the parenting role and taking over her ego functioning temporarily. Once she regained a sense of reality, he assisted her with the practical tasks of adjusting to a life without the loved ones she had lost.

CONCLUSION

The black pastor in the above case study assumed a parenting role. Tradition had given him the opportunity for this. The pastor's willingness to assume such a role temporarily helped to sustain and support Mrs. Smith in her crisis. Moreoever, the pastor drew upon many of the caring resources of the church to support and sustain Mrs. Smith in her crisis.

While I have encountered many examples of the successful use of this parenting role by black pastors, I must, nonetheless, caution that there is a real danger in assuming such a role. It does encourage a degree of dependency on the part of the parishioner. Moreover, it could become a real source of ego gratification for the pastor, and he or she may not be willing to relinquish the parenting role.

What this case study shows is that it is possible to take charge and even take over temporarily without destroying the person's ability to be responsible for his or her own life. Parenting shows care and love, and more pastors in parishes could be more active in parenting without doing great harm. However, the parenting role should be assumed only out of the awareness of the needs of the parishioner and not out of the needs of the pastor.

III
THE SYMBOLIC GUIDING
FUNCTION:
THE CRISIS OF ILLNESS

As a symbol in the black church, the black pastor provided affirmation of the fellowship's identity, its purposes, its values, and its goals. The black pastor inherited his or her function out of a matrix of social and historical cicumstances that made the pastor unique in the entire community. As a symbol, the pastor was supposed to help make life meaningful for the souls under his or her care. As a result of this function, the pastor was expected to help the congregation and the persons within the congregation to make sense out of chaotic experiences that made life frustrating. The pastor's task in the care of souls was to bring to bear upon black persons in crisis the ideas and values that traditionally enabled black people to survive in a world of hostility and oppression.

Many students come to the seminary where I work realizing their symbolic function. They have learned through observation and experience their role to help persons integrate what is happening in their lives into a meaningful purpose that gives them direction. From a practical viewpoint, the students manifest their symbolic guiding function by attempting to provide practical solutions to people's problems. Often this is done by providing a theological rationale for the problem with the hope that the person will find something in it that would provide unity in his or her chaotic life. Of course, there are many drawbacks to this form of guidance, such as imposing a rationale that ignores the personal feelings of the person in crisis and preaching when the pastor really does not know what to do.

Despite the apparent pejorative influences the symbolic guiding function may have upon the parishioner, there are many positive influences that this symbolic function has for guiding in pastoral care. By virtue of the black pastor's symbolic role, he or she is in a position to positively influence the way in which a person in crisis faces the crisis, helping the person mobilize his or her inner resources for problem solving. Many mature black pastors can use their symbolic authority over a person's life without abusing it by patronizing the person or treating the person like a child. They are able to stimulate and facilitate the growth of their parishioners toward personal responsibility through the use of their symbolic role. A case that reflects the positive use of the symbolic role in guidance is presented below. For our purposes, symbolic guidance means the bringing to bear upon the person in crisis the pastor's symbolic significance in such a way that it influences the person's choice of healthy mechanisms for coping with a crisis.

THE CASE STUDY

In the following verbatim, the letter "C" refers to the pastor and the letter "P" refers to the patient.

The case study is of a sixty-two-year-old woman who is in the hospital for an illness that prohibits her from walking. The patient is having problems adjusting to her condition. The pastor does not know whether the impairment to the patient's capacity to walk is temporary.

C_1: Good evening; how are you feeling today?

P_1: Well, I guess I'm all right.

P_2: You look like a minister; are you?

C_2: Yes I am; I am Rev. _____ from the chaplain's office. I have been assigned to this ward, and I will be coming by to see you from time to time.

I have no idea what a typical minister looks like. Perhaps it was the chaplain's dress or the way he carried himself that triggered the woman's remark. Nonetheless, certain factors are already at work concerning the woman's learned expectations about black ministers. Through her raising the question of the professional identity of the pastor, she was transmitting a message to the pastor concerning what she had learned culturally to expect from black ministers. In the following exchanges, you will be able to see the development of the woman's expectation:

P$_3$: Oh yes, please come; I need prayer.

C$_3$: Would you like for me to pray with you?

P$_4$: Yes, please; God is all I have to talk to, and I need to tell him about my troubles.
(The minister prayed with the woman.)

One of the rules I try to follow is to refrain from assuming that I know why a person wants prayer. Moreover, my training, which has been mostly in white institutions, has taught me to look for the unexpressed feeling (in nonverbal communication). For example, I would have been concerned to explore what the troubles were that she wanted to tell God about and why she felt she had no one to talk to.

Notice, however, that the student minister took a different approach altogether. He assumed he knew what this woman wanted and proceeded to pray. What she wanted became clear to him when she said, "You must be a minister." Thirty-seven years' influence by a particular environment had taught this ministerial student what laypeople from that environment expect from ministers. Thus he knew, from this woman's proclamation of his ministerial status, that she wanted him to provide a practical solution to the walking impairment. The fact that this student minister knew what was expected of him is expressed in the following segment of the verbatim:

C$_5$: If you believe in God, he will do what is best for you.

P$_5$: I believe I will walk again soon, and I am not going to need a stick.

C_6: With God, all things are possible if you believe.
P_6: I know what I feel like; I will walk again.

In the response in C_5, which came directly after the prayer, the pastor seems to be responding from an unknown context. That is, his response is connected to the prayer but its connection is not obvious. However, when the symbolic role of black ministers is considered, the context of his statement is apparent. This woman expected him to provide the practical solution to her problem. She wanted him to be a mediator between herself and God so that God would heal her through him. This expectation was unspoken, but it was very much in the mind of the minister. His practical intuition had been shaped and fashioned by culture, and he had learned his symbolic role well. The pastor's view of his role and the woman's expectation of him were the result of a commonly shared cultural background between the pastor and the patient. The pastor's response and the woman's expectation illustrate the symbolic role of the black pastor in operation in the pastoral interaction. More will be said about the response of the pastor in the next section.

THE METHOD OF PASTORAL CARE

The method of pastoral care used by the pastor was guiding through teaching. In response C_5, the pastor was using his personal faith to teach the age-old theology that God knows what is best for people. He was teaching the woman that perhaps she was manipulating God into what she wanted, rather than being open to what God was already doing for her in her present condition.

Another example of this pastor's teaching orientation is seen in the following exchange:

P₁₁: Well, I wonder why God causes some people to suffer when they try to live right.

C₁₁: Well, that's just his way; sometimes suffering is for the best, but we can't understand it. God's ways are not known to man.

There were a variety of ways the student pastor could have responded to this woman's questions. He could have said something like the following: "You are wondering how God picks those who suffer; you have some real feelings about how God is treating you."

These responses are existential in that they attempt to explore the feeling of the patient. However, the student minister chose to teach ideas rather than to reflect feelings. This is another example of the symbolic guiding function of the black pastor. The black pastor is expected to answer questions directly, to provide solutions to problems, to give perspectives when they are asked for by the patient. In short, the pastor was attempting to provide a meaningful framework through which the patient could discover purpose in her suffering.

EVALUATION

One of the most helpful aspects of the model of clinical pastoral education is that it focuses upon what the student brings to ministry. Some clinical supervisors have as their goal helping the ministerial students to use themselves as healing agents in pastoral care. When we analyze what the black ministerial student brought to the clinical setting, we sense a strong symbolic identity and a strong vertical orientation to God.

Given this student's bent in approaching persons in crises, the most helpful thing the clinical supervisor can do is to help him reflect upon his strong symbolic identity and vertical orientation so that he can use these resources to help the parishioner. Because of my strong training background in the Rogerian-Freudian orientation, I found myself on several occasions wanting to force this student to be less aggressive and direct and to be more oriented toward feelings than ideas. However, I was reminded by a colleague that this was not what the student brought to the clinical seminar. Moreover, I was not being true to my own pastoral identity and vertical orientation, which I inherited from my black Christian background and upbringing. Therefore, my style of supervision became oriented toward helping the student develop timing, helping him know when to use his orientation, based upon an awareness of the patient's needs.

One of the most helpful things the student pastor did was to resist being manipulated into playing God. He did not know nor did he pretend to know why the innocent suffered. I am sure the sick woman expected him to try to answer the question, but the pastor was very much aware of his limitations. He could have explored her own bewilderment and disappointment about not finding an answer in greater depth; however, in any case, the patient seemed satisfied with the response and the attentive concern of the pastor.

Throughout this verbatim, the symbolic function of the pastor was operative. However, he resisted the invitation to be omniscient. He did attempt to help clarify the confusion in the lady's mind. His teaching, and the lady's passive acceptance of his teaching about God, were consonant with the symbolic function of the black pastor. He was using his role to help guide the patient into a meaningful and realisic approach to her suffering. Therefore, the minister's guidance helped the patient to face realistically her illness instead of avoiding it through an unrealistic hope. In this way he was using his symbolic role to facilitate healthy crisis coping.

IV
PREACHING AS GUIDING

Because the black pastor has been the symbolic leader of the church, the preaching function has been very important in the pastoral care of black people. In worship, the black pastor used the pulpit to help people find meaning for their existence. The preacher provided the theological world view upon which people could draw to flnd sustenance and guidance for their lives. In this context—when preaching has as its primary aim the care and concern for the person in crisis—this is pastoral care. Through the sermon, the black pastor has often brought the preaching resources to bear upon the lives of persons in difficulty so that they might choose healthy crisis-coping skills.

In the introductory chapter to this book, I pointed out that worship has been a tremendous therapeutic resource for black people. Many negative emotions associated with the frustration of ambitions and goals because of oppression could be expressed in the context of community acceptance. Worship was a socially sanctioned outlet for negative feelings, and as such it contributed to the mental health of the black person. The therapeutic context of black worship, and the black preacher as the major symbol of the church, combined to form a powerful context for the sustaining and guiding ministry of pastoral care.

Such a compatible relationship between the pastor and the congregation existed in the black funeral service. In the funeral, the whole congregation and the minister created a context in which grieving could take place. The grief sufferer did not have to feel ashamed of crying or wailing. The pastor created the context, and the singing of the congregation provided the atmosphere. Through the leadership of the minister, the bereaved family and the congregation grieved corporately.

This chapter will explore the role of preaching in the guiding function. More specifically it will illustrate how a black pastor uses his preaching function in worship to facilitate the grieving process. Prior to this, experiences and characteristics of black funeral practices will be presented.

The outstanding fact in the legacy of the black experience is that death remained a conscious part of the everyday life of black people wthout denial or repression. Commenting on the slave experience, Howard Thurman says:

Death was a fact, inescapable, persistent. For the slave, it was extremely compelling because of the cheapness with which his life was regarded. The slave was a tool, a thing, a utility, a commodity, but he was not a person. He was faced constantly with the imminent threat of death, of which the terrible overseer was the symbol; and the awareness that he (the slave) was only chattel property, the dramatization.[1]

Realism about death was not just confined to the slave; it permeates the black person's life even today. The black person experiences a deep reverence for history and for what has gone before. As in African religions, what those now dead contributed while they were living is always remembered, and that contribution provides a sense of continuity in the present. Reverence for the dead is also seen in black family reunions, where it is customary for black persons to visit the graves of their ancestors.[2] Moreover, reverence for the dead is seen in the emphasis upon proper ceremony and custom in black funeral practices as a way of honoring the dead.[3] It may be concluded, then, that the importance of ancestors and their proper place in the present life of the community help to keep the fact of death inescapably before the conscious minds of black people.

Other legacies of the past which relate to the importance of death in black experiences must also be mentioned here. These include the actual funeral practices of the past which remain in existence today. One such legacy is the practice of delayed funerals. The delayed funeral is characterized by the separation of the funeral from the actual time of death by a period of time often involving several weeks. This practice allows for proper arrangements to be made and for the gathering of the entire family from across the country.[4]

Moreover, such delay involves an emphasis upon the role of proper mourning, which has been characterized by public, vocal expressions of grief.[5]

It is important also to mention the manner in which the life and characteristics of the dead are frankly evaluated at the funeral service by those who came in contact with the person during life. This particular practice has been traced to West African rituals and continues to be practiced in America today. This evaluation, pastoral view of God, African motor-rhythmic patterns, and emotional mourning at funeral services are important therapeutic resources for pastoral care in the black church. Indeed, it is through such traditions that black people have learned to accept death as part of life and as a natural phenomenon which must not be denied or repressed.[6]

A CASE STUDY

In the case study below, the educational role of the black pastor in pastoral care will be emphasized. We shall examine how the black preacher, as a shepherding preacher, has been able to use the sermon and the proclamation of the word to facilitate the grief process.

One day I received a telephone call from a colleague. He was very upset because a young boy whom he had watched growing up had been shot and killed. He said he had grown very close to the boy and his family over the years, and he was not sure he could conduct the funeral services without being overcome by his feelings of loss. He asked me if I would come to spend some time with him before the funeral and assist him at the funeral. He felt that he needed this kind of support to get him through the service and the burial.

It was obvious to me that my friend was very much shaken by the whole experience. He had told me earlier that the deaths of members of his church bothered him a great deal. He said he felt totally helpless to respond to bereaved people because he did not know what to do. Death was an event that made him feel most inadequate as a minister—it was the one time he was aware of his real limitations.

I accepted his invitation. I went to his home that morning about four hours before the funeral. He was preparing his sermon, and he began to tell me what he would be saying. As he talked to me, he forgot his sermon and began to review his relationship with the boy and how he had taught him in Sunday School and counseled with him at crucial points in the boy's development. He said the boy was like a son to him, and he was like a father to the boy. There were many sad moments as he talked. Time passed very quickly, and before we realized it we had to leave for the church.

During the service, he followed the regular order of worship for funerals. There were the hymns, the prayers, and the scripture readings. The choir sang, and the family's favorite solo was performed. Then it came time for the sermon. My friend entitled his sermon "Facing the Shadow of Death Without Fear." I will quote portions from his sermon:

This is perhaps the hardest time in our congregation. Death has cast a dark cloud over us. It has blocked out the sunlight from our lives. It has robbed us of our daylight. It has snuffed out the life of one of our youth.

I could not believe the words that Tommy's mother uttered to me on that tragic day. My heart plunged to the bottom of my chest cavity when she cried out, "They have killed my boy." I found myself gasping for breath with stunned disbelief, hoping that there was some mistake. But there was no mistake. I was hoping that destiny was playing a cruel trick on us all. But there was no trick. Tommy was dead. His life was snuffed out from him for no reason at all. He was just a young man with all his life ahead of him.

We are very fearful today of what death can do to us. We were going along, very happy. We were celebrating how successful we had been in our recent financial campaign. We baptized and read into membership more people than we had since my tenure here. Then all of a sudden, death came along. It raised its ugly head. It asserted its power over our lives. It dashed the gleam from our eyes, and stole our happiness from us.

Yes, death is to be feared. Yes, we fear death because we have no control over it. Tommy had no control over it. I am sure he had no idea that someone would be so desperate for money that they would take his life for it, but they did. Now all of us are fearful of what death can do. We are at the lowest point in the valley today, and it is death's fault. We are angry at death, because we are helpless to do anything about it. Yes, we are very fearful about what death has done and can do.

We are Christians, however, and we believe that there is something more powerful than death. We believe that there is a higher and stronger power that is able to wrestle death to the mat and hold it down for the count of three. Yes, we believe that death has a word, but not the last word. Only God has the last word. God is Alpha and Omega, the beginning and the end.

We do not fear what death can do this afternoon because our God is with us. He has entered the hell of our lives and is working to help us fill the void left in our lives by Tommy's death. Yes, though I walk through the valley of death this afternoon, I will fear no evil, for thou art with me.

61

ANALYSIS OF THE SERMON

One would have had to be in the congregation to appreciate what was going on. What my friend was actually doing was setting an example for the congregation to follow in handling their grief. He was putting his own sorrow into words. He was talking about the fear he had in his own heart of death. He was guiding the congregation and the bereaved persons through their grief by talking frankly about his own feelings of loss. He was saying to them. Follow me; I will show you how to grieve.

In grief work, the essential task is to accept the fact that the deceased has gone, never to return. This is accomplished by reviewing one's relationship with the deceased and experiencing and expressing negative feeling such as fear, anger, guilt, and remorse. Expressing the feelings of loss helps the person to let go of the deceased and return to a meaningful life again. This was actually what my friend was doing. More than this, he was helping the congregation as a corporate community to go through the grief process. They identified with his example as he spoke. They could identify with his example because he put their feelings into words. As he spoke, he became his congregation, and his congregation became him. With his every word, they responded as if to say, This is how I am feeling right now. Some wept, some nodded their heads, and others responded with actual words to what the minister was saying. He was leading as well as teaching them how to grieve.

I conclude that all the elements of good grieving were present in the corporate worship service. There was a review of the events immediately surrounding the death.

There was a corporate expression of the feelings of loss, and Tommy was talked about frankly in the past tense, which indicated the pastor's acceptance of the fact that Tommy was dead. This is how pastoral care is done through worship and preaching.

One of the unique historical aspects of black corporate worship is that the pastor has had the skill to facilitate the expression of real feelings. This ability has been greatly enhanced at times of death by the pastor's frank referral to the deceased person. As pointed out in the last section, the frank evaluation of the life of the deceased helps greatly to facilitate the grieving process.

CONCLUSION

Preaching in corporate worship can be very much a form of pastoral care when its resources are aimed toward those in crisis. In fact, I have known of cases where black ministers have not visited the family before or after the funeral but were nevertheless praised by the bereaved family for having led them through their grief. In these instances, the black pastor was able to show the way to healthy grieving through the sermon and worship. I must add that this is not to negate the importance of calling on the families in the time of bereavement; I am simply pointing out just how important preaching and corporate forms of worship are to black pastoral care.

I would add also the fact that black tradition has provided opportunities for grieving throughout the grief process. All-night wakes prior to the funeral and visits by members of the congregation to the bereaved for weeks following the funeral are examples. Death is taken very seriously; no one should be left to grieve alone. This is the attitude the black church has taken toward death.

This chapter has illustrated that preaching in worship is a form of pastoral care when it is used as a resource for guiding. The black pastor chose to guide his congregation and the bereaved family by showing them how to grieve through this example. He drew upon his own relationship with the deceased to take the worshipers through the bereavement process.

V
THE INDUCTIVE GUIDING FUNCTION: THE PREMARRIAGE CRISIS

As a symbol to the community, the black pastor has been expected to give direction to persons facing crisis. Often the black pastor has been left to his or her own devices to develop meaningful ways of bringing the resources of the church to bear upon pastoral direction. As indicated in the last chapter, one method used by many black pastors has been to draw upon their own experiences as a major resource for giving guidance to persons. Since it took many years to amass the experience necessary to inform the pastor's pastoral care, many parishioners wanted a sea-soned pastor who had experienced life. Often the pastor used trial-and-error methods to develop his or her repertoire of skills in pastoral care, and this meant that he or she became more effective with increasing age. An example of how an elderly black pastor combined his own experience with biblical values to guide a couple will be presented.

It must be added that the pastor's use of a biblical perspective to help persons resolve crises is known as inductive guiding. Inductive guiding seeks to help the person according to wisdom outside both the counselor and the person in crisis.[1]

The following interview is with a seventy-three-year-old pastor whose conversation stimulated much of my thinking concerning the guiding methods of pastoral care. He is retired from the ministry but is still serving part-time with a church.

THE INTERVIEW

Concerning what approach this pastor took in premarital counseling, he stated the following:

1. The first question I ask a couple before they get married is, What is the foundation of a happy and enduring home? Of course, some of them come to it almost immediately, and some beat around the bush and never quite answer the question. Some say getting along with each other. Finally, if they do not get it themselves, I tell them.

2. I tell them that the foundation of a happy and enduring marriage is love and loyalty alone. When things go haywire, then there is something in love and loyalty to

fall back upon. If they build their marriage on financial considerations alone, for example, there is nothing to support the marriage when the couple suffers hard times.

3. The next question I ask is where is their loyalty. In my own pastoral experience, this is the place where a marriage has its difficulty. Many couples don't know their first loyalty. Some of them say their first loyalty is to their mother. Here again, I tell them if they are not able to answer the question. I tell them that their first loyalty is to each other, and they should not let their mother, father, sister, or brother come between them as husband and wife. As a couple, they will no longer be two individual people; rather they will become one. I warn them that their relatives and friends will interfere, and they must be very sure that their loyalty is to each other.

4. I then ask them questions about their finances, trying to find out the kinds of living arrangements they are making. I do this to find out if they would be living with their parents. I then explain to them the dangers of such an arrangement, which are similar to what I have earlier stated about parents and relatives. I tell them that it is best to get their own quarters separate from their parents and relatives.

5. I try to find out if the soon-to-be-married couple is aware of the conflicts they will have in marriage. I ask them where they will turn if they have a problem that they cannot solve by sitting down in conversation to solve a problem that has lasted more than a week. Many of them said they would turn to friends and parents for advice. I warned them that turning to relatives and friends often causes more harm than good, because parents and relatives take sides. I told them they needed to seek a person trained in marriage

counseling. They needed to go to a pastor who is trained or to a professional person in marriage counseling. Trained people lead you to find your own answers to problems and they do not give the wrong [unprofessional] advice.

6. I developed my approach to premarriage counseling from my own experience. I have had to deal with interference from my own relatives into my marriage, and I have had many couples in for counseling where this is the problem. I also found help in forming my views from the biblical reference to couples cleaving to each other and from the marriage ritual of my denomination.

ANALYSIS

In paragraph six of the interview, the pastor explained how he formulated his approach to premarriage counseling. He pointed out the role that his own experience played as well as his understanding of the Bible and the marriage ritual.[2] His own experience and his own methods for solving his own difficulties with relatives became the basic source of his pastoral care. The Bible and the marriage service gave normative support of his experience. The pastor's drawing upon his own experience and biblical tradition was customary for black pastoral care. That is, he had no behavioral models to draw upon that were adequate for his needs. His approach was illustrative of inductive guidance in historical pastoral care.

Another characteristic of black pastoral care is the teaching method. This method was used by this pastor in premarriage counseling. He would begin the session with a series of questions. Once he had listened to the responses, he followed up with the appropriate didactic response suggesting the appropriate answer to the posed question. In general, he was teaching the couple what to expect in marriage and how to respond to future marital events when they happened.

Besides teaching, there were other methods of pastoral care used by this pastor. For example, he used some diagnostic exercises. He used the couple's responses to the questions to ascertain what strengths the couple had. The assessment of strengths basically had to do with the couple's practical, common-sense thinking. If the couple lacked sufficient levels of practical common sense, the pastor corrected the situation by providing the proper knowledge. Here again, underlying the pastor's counseling approach was the behavioral-learning orientation.

The pastor also had to utilize listening skills in approaching couples. He always began with what the couple brought with them in the way of practical sense. He never assumed anything, nor did he begin to teach right away. He listened first to what the couple presented. Then, and only then, did he proceed with the teaching. In this way, the pastor could tailor his approach to the individual needs of the clients.

The way in which this pastor practiced pastoral care reflected the direct guidance approach. His method of pastoral care gave direction in that it sought to lead couples from a state of singleness to a state of marriage. He was seeking to help them make the transition as smoothly as possible. He recognized many changes in the journey of marriage and provided a road map of some of the dangerous curves on the journey. I call this form of direction prepratory guidance. Preparatory guidance correlates with and illustrates the essential symbolic role of the black pastor in pastoral care.

In his preparatory guidance, the minister had a systems orientation to family living. (Chapters 7 and 8 of Part II will explore the boundary approach to marriage counseling.) He perceived the couple not as two individuals who functioned separately, but as part of a unitary system that had to perform certain given functions without interference from outside. The pastor's commitment was to the family as a unit, and he relied on his own experience, biblical norms, and church tradition as his foundation.

The pastor's own wisdom, informed by biblical and church tradition, shows a basic experiential, practical approach to premarriage counseling. His approach, seeking to protect the integrity of the husband-and-wife unit from outside interferences, coincided with a carefully worked out, scientifically formulated theory called structural family therapy. But this pastor did not have the benefit of formal training in such theory. He had to rely on his own experience. In my mind, this affirms that common-sense experience validates theory. In general, I would conclude that black pastors have committed themselves to an approach not because they have heard that it was scientifically valid but because it has worked.[3]

§

PART II

Whereas the intention in Part I was to examine the historical nature of pastoral care in the black church, the purpose of Part II is to develop a model of pastoral care that reflects the changing conditions in the black community and the black church. It was pointed out in Part I that the social conditions that propelled the black minister to the center of the community have changed owing to increased opportunities in American society for black people. The central role of the pastor and support systems in the black church and community has been declining. A model that will design a ministry to persons and families in crisis will be developed reflecting the social realities of the black community today and the contributions of the behavioral sciences.

In Part II, guiding and sustaining will still be the dominant modes of pastoral care emphasized. However, the church's ministry of worship, care, nurturing, and witnessing will be examined in terms of its contribution to the care of persons. Healing and reconciling will not be emphasized as major modes of the model of pastoral care, although healing and reconciling may indeed result from the guiding and sustaining ministries. The pastor's role as sustainer and guide for persons in crises will be the major focus.

VI
A MODEL FOR PASTORAL CARE

In Part I of this book, certain significant insights emerged concerning the function of pastoral care in black churches. Pastoral care has included not only the work of pastors, but the work of the laity. Sustaining and guiding, which involve the corporate sustaining resources of the church and the symbolic leadership role of the black pastor, have been the major functions performed in pastoral care traditionally. These traditions will serve as a foundation for building a model of pastoral care for black churches.

THEOLOGICAL NORMS OF
BLACK PASTORAL CARE

A model for pastoral care must begin with a theological base. If it does not, it will resemble a tree without roots. Without roots, a tree will slowly dry up and die. Analogously, a model of pastoral care without roots in theology will slowly die because it has no foundation.

Black pastoral care has been a response pattern to God's love. It is rooted in God's actions toward persons. Therefore, the basis of black pastoral care has been theological—that is, it has been rooted in black Christians' understanding of the Christian message and their attempt to live this understanding in service to others.

Liberation will serve as the norm upon which a model of pastoral care will be based. Numerous black Christians have understood the gospel in terms of the liberation of persons from oppressive forces in society. Some thinkers see liberation in terms of freeing the oppressed by a radical transformation of social and political structures. Others see liberation as needed not only in the social and political arena, but also in the lives of individuals—the freeing of the self. In this context, the model of pastoral care will be based upon a model of liberation that emphasizes personal as well as social transformation. For our purposes, then, liberation as a norm for pastoral care refers to the freeing of persons from those internal and external forces that prevent them from moving toward their full potential as self-actualizing, assertive human beings related to God. Pastoral care in the context of liberation means the bringing to bear upon a person or family in crisis the total liberation resource of the church.

The norm of liberation has specific implications for the four functions of pastoral care. The ultimate aim of liberation serves the ends of the healing and reconciling aspects of pastoral care more than it does the sustaining and guiding functions. That is, the goal of liberation is to restore persons to wholeness and mend broken relationships with God and with persons.

Although the ultimate aim of liberation is healing and reconciliation, guiding and sustaining will be the major functions used in building the model of pastoral care. For our purposes, healing and reconciling will remain goals of liberation rather than functions of pastoral care. The end result of all pastoral care, then, is the liberation of persons so that they can become whole persons related significantly to God. The sustaining and guiding functions will serve in achieving this ultimate goal.

Not only is liberation the aim of pastoral care; God's liberation activity in Jesus is the foundation of the sustaining and guiding functions of pastoral care. The source of all care is God, and it is through God's liberating acts in Jesus that sustaining and guiding are made possible. Through God's liberation power, the caring community and the pastor can carry out sustaining and guiding ministries. Sustaining and guiding mediate God's liberation activity to persons in crises.

BLACK PASTORAL CARE AND BEHAVIORAL SCIENCE MODELS

The sustaining and guiding functions of black pastoral care are the beginning points for fashioning a model of pastoral care for the black church. The next step in building the model is to examine the relevance of the theories and methods of behavioral science to these functions. The reason for the second step is contained in a statement by my colleague Dr. Thomas J. Pugh.

> Many of the older black pastors have been very sure about their role in pastoral care. However, many of the younger pastors are in a period of transition. They see some of the problems that the old model has, yet they are not sure what models to adopt.[1]

My own bias is that there is a need to pay close attention to the transition phase in black pastoral care. Many of the conditions that have given nourishment to black pastoral care are changing; so are black laymen and black pastors. Future black pastoral care must not only reflect the past; it must also reflect the fact that black ministers and laypersons are increasingly expecting future pastors to be better equipped than in the past.[2] Because of the black revolution, the educational level of the laity has improved. The black minister therefore cannot rely on his or her office to command leadership in the black church as in the past. More and more, churches are expecting the black pastor to bring increased skills and education to the pastoral office; so the black pastor cannot rely upon his or her symbolic significance alone for leadership. There needs to be a bridge between past models and present realities in black pastoral care.

To the end of bridging the past and the present, two behavioral science models appear to be particularly relevant to black pastoral care. These models are systems theory and crisis theory. Both reflect a concern for the wholeness of persons and enable the black pastor and the black church to use the riches of the past for a liberation ministry of pastoral care. The following chart reflects the correspondence between black pastoral care and systems and crisis theories.

DIAGRAM OF CORRESPONDENCE
(Figure 1)

Black Pastoral Care	Behavioral Sciences
1. Rooted in God's activity	1. Emphasis on spiritual resources
2. Concern over the impact of racism on the black personality	2. Concern for changing social forces which hinder personality growth
3. Using corporate supportive systems	3. Emphasis upon support systems
4. The role of black pastor: Guiding	4. The Role of Practitioner: Active problem-solving approaches to persons and families
Sustaining	Support of persons During life crisis
Active	Active change agent
Educational	Educational approaches to persons and family
Taking charge	Taking charge in family counseling
Diagnosis of problems and tasks	Diagnosis of problems and tasks

As you can see in the above chart, there is some correspondence between black pastoral care and systems and crisis theories. According to the diagram, there is a real possibility that systems and crisis theories may serve the ends of black pastoral care. The model for pastoral care developed in this chapter will pick from the behavioral sciences those concepts and functions that serve the ends of black pastoral care.

If the similarities between black pastoral care and systems and crisis theories are to be utilized in fashioning the model, these two behavioral science theories must serve the end of liberation. Black pastoral care is a liberating response to what God has done, and systems and crisis theories must be grafted onto this response. A crisis is an obstacle in the way of a person's achieving his or her life goals that is temporarily insurmountable and unamenable to customary methods of problem-solving. A crisis represents a turning point, and the person can either move toward further growth and development or reverse his or her growth process. In the context of liberation, a crisis is not only a turning point for increased growth or deterioration, it is a potential period of *Kairos*—that is, a period when the liberating powers of God can break into the person's life to move him or her toward personal development of self and growth toward others and God. When crisis theory is applied toward the goal of liberation, its intent changes; it has the potential for serving the ends of God's liberating ministry as well as personal growth.

Systems theory may likewise serve the end of liberation. Systems theory is an attempt to organize the data of experience into a dynamic, complex, and interacting whole. The basic intent of systems theory and methods is to produce well-integrated and functioning persons. The goal of systems theory, as visualized within the liberation model, is to enable persons to become integrated, functioning persons whose lives are significantly related to God and others. The goal of systems theory thus becomes more than its original intent.

The model of pastoral care for the black church will emerge from traditional black pastoral care and will borrow from systems and crisis theories. This borrowing from these behavioral science disciplines will serve the ends of liberation.

A MODEL FOR PASTORAL CARE

The proposed model for pastoral care has four functional areas of ministry in which pastoral care will take place. These areas are worship, care, nurture, and witness.[3] Pastoral care takes place in *worship* when needs of persons in crisis situations are addressed. Pastoral care also takes place when persons *care* for the needs of those facing crises in a giving, selfless manner. *Nurturing* pastoral care prepares the congregation to respond to the needs of persons in crisis. Finally, the *witnessing* aspect of pastoral care takes place when the church attempts to change those conditions which prevent persons from choosing healthy crisis-coping patterns.

Worship, nurture, care, and witness represent the total ministry of the church. As such, worship, nurture, and witness are ministries alongside care. However, these three ministries serve the ends of care when their focus is primarily upon the needs of the person in crisis. Therefore, worship, nurture, and witness will be examined in terms of their importance for pastoral care, particularly as related to the sustaining and guiding functions. More precisely, they will be explored as potentials for the pastor to draw upon in the caring ministry of the church.

The following is presented as a model for pastoral care for black churches:

A Model for Pastoral Care

Diagram of a Model of Pastoral Care
(Figure 2)

Worship
(Central)
(Celebration of Liberation)
Values

Translation of Values into Reality		Translation of Values into Reality
Care	Nurture	Witness
Assessing	Educating	Changing social
Sustaining	and training	values and
Guiding	laity	forces
Mobilization of	Utilization of	Prophetic emphasis
resources	symbols and	
	rituals	

The diagram above organizes the model of pastoral care for the black church around the major functional ministries of the church—namely, worshiping, caring, nurturing, and witnessing. Notice that the worshiping task of the church iscentral and the beginning point of the model. Worship is central because there is no church or ministry without worship. Worship gives ministry its *raison d'être,* its reason to be. It lifts up the fact that there would be no Christian church if it were not for God's action toward us in the life, death, and resurrection of Jesus Christ. Therefore, worship is central in the model, because it keeps before the worshiping community the fact of what God has done and continues to do for persons in crisis. Worship addresses what God has done for persons in crisis and helps the congregation to discern its own ministry to persons in crisis. In this light, worship is a potential resource for pastoral care.

God's concern for persons must not only be lifted up in worship; it must also be translated into the reality of the church and the world. The next dimension of ministry following worship is caring. The caring dimension of the model is the transformation of God's concern for persons into concrete reality within the life of the church through the minister's: (1) assessment of the nature of the crises persons confront; (2) guiding and sustaining of persons and families in crisis to facilitate healthy crisis-coping; and (3) actively mobilizing family, extended family, community, and cultural resources for the support of persons in crisis.

Another dimension of translating God's concern for persons into the life of the local church is nurturing. Here, the minister creates an environment within the congregation which reflects the concern of Jesus with liberation. To create this kind of environment, the minister educates and trains the laity for their caring role to persons and families in crisis. This is done through the utilizaton of many of the traditional church symbols and rituals such as baptism, confirmation, marriage, and the funeral service. These rituals and symbols are not just ceremonies in which the laity participates; they can be starting points for introducing the laity to the growth cycle in the human growth process and for helping the laity to understand their ministry to persons throughout the life cycle.

The final dimension of the model is the witnessing component. The liberation ministry of the church needs to go beyond the local church in an effort to change the impact of social values and social forces on the lives of persons in crisis. This ministry is accomplished through many of the prophetic strategies used in the black church historically, including lobbying, community organization, and advocacy.

The pastoral care model outlined in the preceeding paragraphs draws upon broad categories of ministry for its development. These broad categories are designed to serve the ends of pastoral care in the model. In addition, the model is holistic in that it addresses the needs of persons individually and corporatively. Beyond this, it addresses the social factors influencing the lives of persons.

THE CARING MINISTRY OF THE BLACK CHURCH

In the model of pastoral care outlined above, crisis theory is drawn upon to help one understand the needs of persons. Crisis theory points out the various situational and developmental crises that people face in the drama of human growth. Situational crises are those in which persons face actual loss or threats of loss resulting from many external environmental factors—for example, accidents, natural disasters, moving, and death of a loved one. On the other hand, developmental crises happen within persons owing to the natural process of human growth—for example, birth, childhood, adolescence, marriage, middle age, and old age. Situational crises and developmental crises, then, help the model of pastoral care for the black church focus on human needs. In this way, the model brings together theology and psychology in a meaningful way.

Diagram of Types of Crises

Developmental Crises	Situational Crises
Child entering school for first time	Loss of Limb
Onset of adolescence	Natural disaster
Entrance to college	Car accident
Getting married	Illness
Birth of a child	Relocation or moving
Onset of middle age	
Onset of old age	
Death	

In the caring ministry, there are many resources within the tradition of the church on which the pastor can draw to sustain persons when they face situational and developmental crises. The black church has had many such support systems to help persons maintain emotional and physical integrity during crises. In this model of pastoral care, the black pastor must draw upon these support systems as well as crisis theory.

Support systems are patterns of continuous ties among significant persons that help those in crisis to maintain psychological and physical integrity. In the black church, these support systems include black worship, characterized by African rhythmic patterns, which have supplied a socially sanctioned outlet for the release of deep emotions. Also, the black church has provided a value system and a consistent world view which have undergirded the attempt of black people to find meaning in life in spite of the situational crises in which they found themselves. Such caring groups as the prayer meeting and burial societies have also been important in helping persons deal with life crises. Rituals such as baptismal and funeral rites have assisted black persons with developmental crises. All these support systems are resources that have informed the unique nature of pastoral care in the black church. These resources for care must be used by the pastor when attempting to meet the needs of people in crisis.

Black Church Support Systems Diagram

Black Worship
Black World View
Care Groups
(prayer meeting and burial society)
Rituals
(baptism and funeral)

In the model of pastoral care, the caring dimensions of the minister's role are to diagnose the nature of the crisis, intervene in the lives of persons in crisis, and to mobilize the many support systems within the family and the church. The particular dimensions of these roles will be examined briefly.

From a diagnostic point of view, the minister must be aware of all the system influences upon the persons in crisis situations. Therefore, the minister needs to be aware of: (1) the nature of the crisis; (2) the personal resources of the person and family for responding to the crisis; (3) the resources within the social network for support to persons in crisis; (4) the resources within the community for support to persons in crisis; and (5) the resources within the local church for support to persons in crisis. (See Figure 5 for an example of various systems that influence persons in crises.) The purpose of such an assessment of these varied systems is to develop a plan for intervening in the lives of persons undergoing crises. This assessment is necessary for mobilizing the resources within the social network, community, and church for caring for persons in crisis.

Diagram of Systems Influencing Person in Crisis (Figure 5)

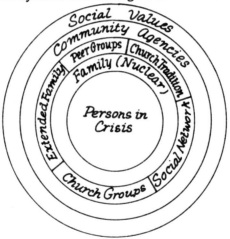

In assessing the resources for assisting the person in crisis, the black minister must draw upon black church traditions (see Figure 4). It is precisely in the mobilization of its support systems resources that the genius of the black church can be exploited. The strength of the black church from a systems perspective has been its consistent use of systems in crisis intervention. The black minister, as a diagnostician, tries to assess these various systems (see Figure 5).

Assessing the nature of the resources is important, because the pastor must choose how he or she will intervene in the lives of persons to sustain and guide them through crises. It may be possible for the minister to use all the systems outlined in Figure 5 at different points during a crisis. Therefore, a systematic understanding of the role of systems and their importance during crisis periods is a tremendous asset to the caring ministry of the church.

A NURTURING MINISTRY

In the model of pastoral care, the third dimension is the nurturing ministry. This aspect of the model focuses upon the black pastor's training the laity for its ministry to persons in life crises. Training and education of the laity for its ministry is extremely important in developing a systems approach to crisis intervention. This is because the laity plays an important role in support systems, and it must know the needs of the persons in crisis as well as the tasks that need to be done to foster healthy crisis-coping.

In training persons for their caring tasks to others, it is important to keep in mind the developmental crisis outlined in Figure 3 and the black church resources outlined in Figure 4. Crisis theory and black church resources can be used together in forming a base to train the laity. For example, the black church has traditions that have dealt with birth, adolescence, marriage, and old age. Therefore, the pastor's understanding of the various stages of the life cycle and its resources can be drawn upon in the nurturing ministry. It is important to turn to some examples.

Birth as a Life Crisis

Pregnancy is a crisis because it causes disequilibrium, emotional upset, role changes, and communication difficulties within the family. Moreover, the problem-solving mechanisms of the family and of the expectant mother are altered because of certain metabolic changes occurring inside the mother, even though they are normal occurrences in pregnant women. Often, these changes create moods within the mother that cause tension between her and her husband.

The crisis period continues when the child is born, but then the child's needs become the focus of the crisis. When the child is born, he or she needs an atmoshere of trust in order to grow and develop according to a normal maturation pattern. It is crucial that the infant experience this sense of basic trust in the first years of life, because the child's future identity is built upon the trust that has been experienced in the first years of existence. Moreover, the care and support that the mother experiences during pregnancy and during the early years of the child's life enable her to communicate warmth to the child, which is essential if the child is to experience a sense of basic trust.

The black pastor needs to prepare the congregation for its role in dealing with expectant parents and with parents with small infants. In training the laity for its ministry to these parents, the black pastor can draw upon the tradition of adoption existent in the black community and in the black church. The uniqueness of black adoption lies in the fact that it was not conceived of as a legal formality, but that it was a response to what the black community saw as its responsibility as defined by social custom.[4] In black adoption practices, relatives and friends cared for the parentless, the homeless, and the so-called illegitimate children in the community. The community saw as its responsibility the care of every child, and thus it was customary to incorporate orphan children into the family and treat them as part of the natural family.

The adoption practices in the black community are remnants of the African heritage of the extended family. The extended family in Africa refers to two or more blood relatives living in the same household or neighborhood.[5] In Africa and in the United States, it has been the practice of extended families to care for any and all children that were related to the family. Beyond this, it was the responsibility of the whole tribe to care for its member children. That these practices have continued in America is demonstrated in the many black churches that have been comprised of several extended families.

The black pastor can draw upon black adoption practices and extended family resources when training the laity about its role in caring for prospective mothers and fathers in the black church. These traditions of adoption and extended family form natural building blocks for incorporating a training program in the caring ministry of the black church during the life crisis of birth. The nurturing ministry may also inform training for meeting the psychological needs of the mother, father, and the expected child. Moreover, this tradition can be drawn upon in order to assist the training of the laity in performing extended family and parenting roles for children. These roles are symbolized through the dedication and infant baptismal services in the black church.

In summary, the adoption tradition in the black community presents an important resource upon which the black pastor can draw in training the laity to care for expectant parents and families with small children.

Adolescence as a Crisis

Adolescence is a trying transitional period between childhood and adulthood brought about by the psychological and physical changes taking place in the young person. This is the period of identity formation in which the individual learns who he or she is apart from others and finds his or her place in the world through developing the kinds of skills necessary for social and economic well-being. Traditionally, this transition has been difficult for black youth because of political disfranchisement, economic exploitation, negative attitudes toward blacks in the wider culture, and the instability of some black families.

Heretofore, the black church has been very inadequate in its ministry to youth[6] and therefore has no real tradition to rely upon in its nurturing ministry to youth. However, the black church can explore the functions that African initiation rites performed in helping the adolescent in the transition from childhood to adulthood. Moreover, the black church needs to explore the traditional practice of confirmation, a service in which the youth is initiated into the church. In confirmation, the laity performs an important function of accepting the youth into the church, thus symbolizing the fact that he or she has gone through a period of training and is now ready to take on adult Christian responsibility. The importance of confirmation in the nurturing ministry of the black church should not be underemphasized; indeed, the black minister needs to mobilize this resource to aid black youth in their struggle for identity. In those traditions where confirmation is not practiced, adult baptism as a symbol should be explored for its potential contribution to the nurturing ministry of the black church to youth.

Marriage as a Crisis

Marriage is problematic for many young black adults. The legacy of the break-up of the black family during slavery, and the subsequent economic, social, and political forces that have perpetuated the break-up of the black family even today, have made the formation of stable families in certain segments of the black community difficult. However, the black church has traditionally provided a value base upon which unstable black families could build.[7] Also, the extended-family concept exhibited in many black churches has helped to bring stability to the family life of the black community. The task of helping train the black laity for its ministry in the crisis of marriage can be facilitated by drawing upon the traditional role of the black church, which has provided a stable family life for black people when otherwise there would have been no stable family life.

In the following chapter, black family life will be examined in greater detail.

Old Age and Retirement as a Crisis

At the onset of old age, many psychological and physical changes are taking place or have already taken place within the aging person. The basic task during this period is for the aging person to find new meaning and value in life in a society that emphasizes the benefits of staying young.

Fortunately, the black church has a tradition that emphasizes the importance of the elderly in the life of the church. Carried over from the African past, the tradition of respect for ancestors has influenced the attitudes of black persons toward the role of the elderly in the total life of the community. According to Herskovits, respect for elders among the slaves was a matter of social code inherited from Africa,[8] and this respect was shown by the practice of calling all older persons by the terms of "uncle" and "aunty" whether they were relatives or not.[9] This custom is still practiced in my own experience. It was considered bad luck to sass older persons; younger persons would also turn their heads or avert eye contact with the elders out of respect, according to Herskovits.[10] Herskovits concludes that this respect for elders has been carried over into the black church through preaching accompanied by assents or spontaneous expressions from the congregation, such as "Yes, Lord," in accordance with the minister's age and rank in the community.[11]

The black pastor, then, has a rich tradition upon which to build in educating the laity concerning the needs of the elderly. Using African and black church traditions, he or she can enable the laity to appreciate the value and worth of the aged and assist the laity in helping the aged within the congregation to find meaning for their lives through the program of the church.

We have examined the crisis of birth, adolescence, marriage, and old age in relation to the nurturing ministry. Bereavement as a crisis was omitted, having been examined in chapter 3. It must be emphasized that crises present opportunities to the black church and its pastor for ministering to persons, primarily because persons are open to the influence of others during crisis periods more than at any other time in their lives. Moreover, crises present opportunities for the black church to draw upon its traditions in assisting in the nurturing task of educating the congregation.

THE WITNESSING MINISTRY
IN THE PROPOSED MODEL

The final dimension of the model of pastoral care is the witnessing ministry in the black church, built upon the prophetic tradition of the black church, which began with Richard Allen and culminated with Dr. Martin Luther King, Jr. In this context, the goal of the witnessing aspect of pastoral care is to transmit the liberation ministry into action not only within the congregation but also in the community by addressing those forces in society that prevent the growth of persons.

In their study, Thomas Pugh and Emily Mudd outline the central issue which the black community must address. Commenting on the subjects of the study, they state:

> One item pertains to the realization of the aspirations of those men and women for themselves and for their children. They seem obsessed by economic need—lack of regular work and adequate income. Hope keeps them alive and lively, for they do not see the end of their struggle. What will happen to their aspirations? As these needs continue unmet, the correlation between a lack of good human relationships and the ablity to cope with personal problems becomes evident.[12]

Pugh and Mudd see economic needs, psychosocial needs, and the ability to adjust to personal problems as linked together. At some point, the witnessing ministry of the black church will have to address the economic factor influencing the development of the black personality. In fact, the witnessing ministry of the black church must address what Caplan refers to as "basic supplies." That is, the black church must work to ensure the basic economic needs of families, to lessen conditions that prevent full participation of all family members in the family, and to lessen environmental influences that hinder the growth of persons within the family.

With regard to economic needs, the black church must attempt to influence the policies of the city, county, state, and federal governments in order to ensure that jobs for minorities exist; that job training is available; and that job discrimination is prosecuted. The goal of such witnessing is to provide some economic security so that parental energies can go into creating an atmosphere of support where the child can develop a basic sense of trust. When the parents must expend most of their concern on their economic survival, much of the energy needed to provide psychosocial support for the child is depleted.

The black church must also address those values in wider society which permit economic exploitation of blacks. These values, which underlie the attitudes and behavior of many non-blacks toward blacks, are too pervasive to include under the rubric of racism alone, although racism is a part of it. These values are related to social-class issues. They are characterized by ethnocentrism (exaggerated group loyalties), and they involve ethnic stereotyping influenced by values centered around the work ethic. The role of the witnessing task of the black church is to hold consistently before society the values inherent in the Constitution, as Dr. Martin Luther King, Jr., was able to do.

Many of the methods of addressing social issues have changed since the civil-rights revolution. More recently the black revolution has adopted the strategies of community organization and community planning. Therefore, the black church must take its witnessing task seriously and become involved in the black community's fight for economic and political lobbying, community organization around selected issues, voter registration, sponsorship of economic ventures, and other means. In this way, the black church can help ensure the basic environment vital to the growth of persons.

SUMMARY

Pastoral care is indeed the ministry of the whole church to persons in crisis. In this chapter, I have sought to outline a model of pastoral care that involves the whole church. Black pastoral care and behavioral sciences have been correlated to construct a model of pastoral care for the black church.

Admittedly, the model developed in this chapter has gone far beyond the traditional notion of healing, sustaining, guiding, and reconciling. However, it must be reiterated that worship, caring nurture, and witnessing are resources that can be brought to bear upon persons and families in crisis. When these resources are employed, the result is rightly called pastoral care.

VII
A LOOK AT A BLACK FAMILY CRISIS

Throughout the history of black people's stay in America, the black family has been under constant bombardment. Slavery had a negative influence upon the black family, because it separated family members from one another. Following slavery, the big migration to Northern cities and severe economic factors split many black families. Throughout the black person's tenure in America, the black family in general has been in need of firm roots in deep soil.

The black church has been the rich soil for the black family. During slavery, Reconstruction, and the great migration, the black church served magnificently as an extended family for persons who had been separated from their families. However, the need for the black church to be a surrogate family in the life of the black community has not changed today. Social factors still indicate that the black church's role relative to the black family is not finished. This is graphically illustrated by the words of Deotis Roberts:

> Martin Luther said to the German people: "If God is your Father, the church is your mother." The black theologian can correctly point to the black church as a family of God for those E. Franklin Frazier refers to as "homeless women and roving men." Separation of families during slavery was followed almost at once by the scattering of families during the migration to urban centers. This has been followed by a welfare system that almost finished off the possibility of a strong family life for blacks. The recovery of a meaningful family life for blacks is one of the greatest challenges facing the black church and its ministry to black people. The task may seem more hopeful if we remember that the black church was a family for blacks when there was no organized family.[1]

Indeed, the recovery of a meaningful family life is still one of the basic tasks of the black church today. The concern of this chapter is to look at the black family in terms of the proposed model for pastoral care. To this end, black pastoral care will be correlated with family systems theory so that the black pastor can approach black families with the uniqueness of his or her heritage, as well as the contributions of the present.

A NATURAL WEDDING

In chapter 5 an interview with a black pastor on premarriage counseling was presented. In that interview, the black pastor explained how he was able to use his own experience and the New Testament norm of spouses leaving their father and mother and cleaving to each other as the foundation of his premarriage counseling. It was suggested at that time that such an approach was the forerunner of what is called boundary theory in family systems theory (see page 70).

Keeping in mind the fact that black ministers today are in a transition period between past and present models, I would suggest that the black minister retain the educative and inductive methodology of the past and explore new methods that help him or her exploit this heritage. In this sense, the pastor will graft new branches onto the tree. The tree remains the same, but the new branches give the tree added life. What I propose to do is to graft a new branch, called boundary theory, onto the tree, represented by the experience of the black pastor presented in chapter 5.

There is a natural wedding between the active educational guidance offered by the black pastor who did premarriage counseling and boundary theory. The black pastor did not hesitate to teach and direct the engaged couple concerning their need to secure their relationship with each other from unnecessary interferences from the outside. Boundary theory—which holds that lines of separation between different family functions should be maintained—provides a philosophical explanation which helps the pastor teach the engaged couple how to maintain their boundary.[2] In summary, boundary theory can help black pastors in using their own experience and knowledge of the scripture in pastoral care, while helping them add to their repertoire of skills.

The methods of boundary family therapy are indeed

active and teaching oriented. They rely upon reenactment of family problems in the presence of the pastor. While the problem is being reenacted, the pastor is assessing how he can help the couple or family secure its lines of demarcation separating family functions. The pastor does this by introducing new styles of relating that teach the couple and/or family to solve its boundary problem.

It is precisely this active teaching orientation which enables the black pastor to continue the active guiding role of the past. The pastor assumes a take-charge posture; but through the reenactment of the problem, the couple and/or family assumes a significant participatory involvement. The pastor directs, but he or she does not take over.

THE TASKS FAMILIES MUST ACCOMPLISH

In this section, an in-depth view of family boundaries will be presented.

Families exist to satisfy some very basic human needs. Families exist to satisfy persons' needs for love and affection, for sex and procreation, and for the rearing and guiding of children. Within the family, there are certain patterns that must be developed in order to meet these basic needs. If these patterns are not developed within the family, the family will not be able to meet its members' needs.

In the family, needs of persons are met when the family maintains its boundaries. Boundaries are those lines which flexibly separate family functions. For example, a husband and wife need to have a sense of who they are as a couple apart from their parents and in-laws and apart from their children. The husband and wife need to work out a degree of intimacy and reciprocal sharing that should not be in any way interfered with by outsiders. This means that the spouses must have a system that is protected from unnecessary intrusions from outside that system. Unnecessary interferences in the spouse subsystem will impair the functioning of the whole family. If the husband and wife cannot meet each other's needs to some degree of satisfation, the whole family crumbles. Therefore, boundaries that protect the husband and wife from unwanted intrusions need to be set in each family. In family systems theory, the way in which families maintain their boundaries between the different subgroupings within the family are called patterns.

Some families have no boundaries at all. They have no distinctions between the spouse subsystem, the child subsystem, or the parent subsystem. The in-laws and the children intrude into the spouse subsystem at will. Parents cannot distinguish their role from their children's role. Perhaps they also cannot distinguish their friends from the children's friends. Such a family has a blurred boundary pattern. At the other extreme is the family whose boundaries are too rigid. No one is allowed to intrude into the different subsystems in the family. Neither the blurred or rigid boundary pattern is adequate. Each family must have secure boundaries, but the boundaries must be flexible. Rigid boundaries are just as bad as no boundaries at all.

In addition to the spouse subsystem in the family, there are two additional subsystems that carry out functions within the nuclear family—the parent and the child subsystems.[3] The function of the parent subsystem is to perform the task of nurturing children in the growth process. Children need recognition for their accomplishment of such things as potty training, walking, speaking, writing, learning, and so forth. They also need to have explained to them why they are rewarded and punished by their parents. These two needs—the recognition of developmental accomplishments and the explanation of the reasons behind discipline—are functions that must be carried out by the parental subsystem. Failure to do so would mean that the children would fail to internalize the rules necessary for them to develop appropriate behavior.

Like the spouse subsystem, the boundaries between the children and parents need to be maintained. Children need parents. Children do not need to become parent to their parents or parents to themselves. Parents must work very hard to keep their children from crossing into the parental role. This can be done by not giving the children parental responsibility. If the spouse subsystem is functioning adequately, children feel secure in being children, and parents feel secure in being parents. However, when the spouse subsystem is not functioning adequately, children often are put in a position of parenting themselves and their parents.

The final task that the family must perform is to help the child learn the social skills necessary to get along in life with others. These social skills are generally learned in the children's peer groups. These peer groups are called child subsystems. This child subsystem also needs to be protected from unecessary intrusions by others. Children need the security that they can choose friends and perform tasks without being overprotected by their parents. Of course, parents have to be concerned about their child's well-being, but parents should learn to differentiate between healthy activity and unhealthy activity among their children's peers. The point here is that children need some time to negotiate life for themselves as part of their growing-up experience.

Boundaries influence the way in which families solve crises. In crisis situations, families that do not have well-functioning subsystems find it difficult to solve their problems. Families with boundaries that are too blurred or too rigid usually meet crisis situations unprepared. They flounder and seem never to solve their problems. They seem to be in a constant state of turmoil.

Below, a case study of a family with inadequate boundaries will be presented to illustrate how a black pastor used boundary theory to understand what was going on in the family.

PRESENTATION OF A CASE ILLUSTRATION

The Jones family consists of Esther Jones, a black female of about thirty years of age; her husband, George, who is thirty-four years old; and four children. There are two boys, whose ages were six and eight at the time of the intervention. There are two girls, whose ages were nine and eleven. Esther and George have been married for eleven years. Esther is a housewife, and George works for the city. His pay is barely over a hundred dollars a week. He also is in partnership with several friends in a clothing store.

Esther and George have lived in a small apartment in the home of his mother since their marriage. George is extremely close to his mother and is inclined to accept her advice rather than his wife's concerning the needs of the children. Likewise, as the landlady, the mother feels she has the right to enter the Joneses' home whenever she deems it necessary. The mother's intrusions form the basis for contantly recurring fights between George and Esther. The involvement of Esther's family is evidenced in the fact that her four brothers and sisters often care for the children when Esther is in need of rest from them.

Violent arguments erupt among all family members. On the one hand, Esther and George engage in arguments that eventuate in threats and counter threats concerning divorce, money, and the children. Such disputes are never resolved; thus, for them, problems seem to worsen rather than to become better. On the other hand, the children also engage in arguments that evolve into physical pushing and shoving. A high noise level results, causing the mother to shout at the children. Finally, the children often become involved in parental disagreements, particularly those centering around them. In these instances, the children often become pawns whom the spouses use to greatest advantage against each other.

Outside the home, the boys are discipline problems, while the girls appear as model children. The acting-out behavior of the boys causes them difficulty in school, and frequent visitations to the school by both parents are made in this regard. While the girls do not exhibit the same problems as their brothers, they nonetheless lack initiative and are constantly dependent upon others for guidance.

Esther came to the pastor, complaining that she feared George had become involved with another woman. The pastor had observed that a great deal of tension existed in the family and was glad Esther was seeking aid from him. He listened very carefully to Esther's story and decided he needed to talk to the husband before trying to figure out the problem. While visiting the home of the Jones family and talking to the husband, each child, and the mother-in-law, he was able to understand the family problem.

The pastor surmised that Esther's unhappiness originated with the intrusions of the mother-in-law into how she wanted to raise her children. Moreover, the pastor pointed out, Esther was jealous of the influence her mother-in-law had over George which she did not have. He felt that this made Esther angry and precipitated many of the fights. He said further that George would respond to his wife's anger at him by withdrawing gradually from the home. It was this withdrawal that the pastor felt triggered Esther's fear that her husband might be having an affair.

The pastor also said that the children got involved in the arguments. Their story, according to the pastor, was that they were very much concerned that their father might become violent with their mother. However, they felt that their mother was too nagging and should back off. The pastor reported that they would intervene in order to try to lessen the loud shouting and bring some degree of reason to the situation.

When the pastor was asked to conceptualize the problem in the family, he said that George needed to find a way to become detached from his mother so that Esther would not have to nag him, and that they both needed to keep the children out of their arguments.

BOUNDARY ANALYSIS

It can be seen in the case presented above that the pastor possessed good diagnostic skills. It may be added here that he had been attending case seminars at a mental health center and was well versed in boundary theory. It would be good to look at the pastor's diagnosis based on boundary theory.

The pastor assumed that the major problem in the family was the blurring of the boundaries—that is, that the family's living in the home of the mother-in-law and the husband's relationship with the mother was the problem. In addition, he assumed that it was not helpful for the children to interfere in the parents' fights. Therefore, his conclusion was that the spouse boundary needed to be strengthened by preventing the mother-in-law and the children from intruding into the husband-wife relationship.

The pastor realized that the family had difficulty solving its problems because of the lack of boundaries in the spouse subsystem. The blurring of the lines made George and Esther avoid the real problem, and that was resolving the conflict between them. They would blame each other rather than try to secure the boundaries of their relationship. Moreover, allowing the children to interfere in their arguments forced the children to choose between their father and mother. This naturally intensified the conflict. Therefore, the pastor felt that the boundary around the family's spouse subsystem had to be closed before the crisis could be resolved.

THE VALUE OF BOUNDARY THEORY
FOR THE BLACK PASTOR

The value of boundary theory from a diagnostic perspective was that it helped the black pastor approach the family with the traditional problem-solving orientation. In Part I, it was pointed out that black pastors have traditionally searched for a problem that could be solved in a practical way. Boundary theory gave this black pastor the same option. Notice how he interviewed every member of the family involved before he made his assessment. In the interviewing process, he was looking for that problem which, when solved, would clear up the conflict in the family. His understanding of boundary theory greatly helped in this process.

Not only did boundary theory help the black pastor find the problem, it also enabled him to set the task that the family must accomplish to solve its problem.

In Part I, it was also pointed out that black pastors seek to find those tasks which can help the families they counsel solve their problems. Boundary theory assists this proclivity to find a task that will be helpful. The task here was to secure the spouse boundary from intrusions.

SUMMARY

In this chapter, I have attempted to illustrate the relevance of boundary theory in family therapy for the black pastor. The emphasis here was upon how boundary theory enabled the black pastor to use his natural orientation toward problem-solving in crisis situations. It was demonstrated that boundary theory could be very useful to black pastors who are problem-solvers.

There was no attempt to demonstrate the relevance of boundary theory to actual problem-solving in this chapter. The emphasis was rather upon the usefulness of boundary theory from a diagnostic perspective. The next chapter will illustrate how this theory helps the black pastor enrich his or her guiding skills.

VIII
FAMILY GUIDING

In black pastoral care, the black minister has been active, task oriented, has used educational methods, and has taken charge. This chapter will illustrate how family boundary theory is useful in helping the black pastor augment the aspects of the guiding orientation. To this end, caring—the second dimension of the proposed model of pastoral care outlined in chapter 6—will be utilized. More specifically, after the assessment of the family problem, actual intervention must take place.

In black pastoral care, the black minister has relied greatly upon his own experience and external norms to guide persons in emotional and family difficulty. I am not suggesting a change in this orientation, but I would like to propose ways in which the black pastor can make greater use of his own experience through applying the boundary theory. I would suggest that the black pastor use his or her experience to: (1) guide the person's reconstruction of the problem, (2) guide the expression of feelings, (3) accomplish the task of problem-solving, and (4) mobilize the family system for change.

These four methods need to be examined in greater detail. In guiding a person to reconstruct the problem, it is important to help him or her isolate the factors leading up to and causing the crisis. The thinking of each person in the family has become disorganized. In this way, the pastor helps the family understand what happened and why it happened. Often, clarification of the problem gives the family hope that finally something can be done.

In helping the family clarify the problem, the black pastor does not sit passively by. He or she can be very active in leading the family to the problem. By active participatory listening, the pastor responds to what the family members say, thereby enabling them to get closer and closer to their problem. In this guiding, the pastor uses active listening as his or her basic method of guiding.

When persons in the family begin to reconstruct the problem, the pastor often encounters diverse feelings. Sometimes the persons feel hopeless, helpless, angry, upset, and overwhelmed by the crisis. The pastor should not bypass the feelings while analyzing and seeking the problem. Ignoring the feeling may communicate to the family members that they do not matter or that they are not worthwhile. Conversely, to acknowledge the feelings expressed helps the family members gain a feeling of being accepted amid self-doubt. Moreoover, accepting feelings helps them focus much more clearly on the problem, because they feel they would not be rejected by the pastor for what they say.

One often uses one's own imagination and experience to recognize feelings. The black pastor who has relied a great deal upon his or her experience in the past can imagine what he or she might be feeling because of having experienced similar circumstances. Using this personal experience to understand the feelings of family members is indispensible in communicating acceptance and respect.

Once the problem is clarified, the pastor must help the family solve its problem in a realistic way. Drawing upon an active problem-solving orientation from black pastoral care, the black pastor can proceed to help the family with its problem. Using such techniques from boundary theory as reenactment of the family problems, the pastor can guide the family to a reslution of the problem.

Finally, the pastor must mobilize the resources within the family for change. Actually, this step includes the third step in the previous paragraph—the application of boundary theory. The pastor should use all the resources available to the family to help in the problem-solving. In this way, the pastor can be consistent with the traditional use of support systems by black pastors.

GUIDING THE FAMILY TO THE PROBLEM

Below is a portion of a verbatim reflecting the pastor's attempt to help the family clarify the problem. This was the first interview where the pastor saw the Jones family together. This case is the same one presented in the last chapter, involving George and Esther.

In the verbatim below, the capital letters symbolize the names of those participating in the counseling sessions. The letter "P" refers to the pastor; "E" refers to Esther; "G" refers to George; "ML" refers to the mother-in-law; and "C" refers to the oldest girl.

P_1: Esther, you came to see me about the problem you feel you have in your marriage. Could you tell me more about this problem?

E_1: Well, it goes back to my husband's new job. He began his new job with the city and at the same time opened this shoe store. Since he began this job at the shoe store, he has been neglecting me. I get the feeling that he thinks I am not good enough for him.

G_1: I never said you weren't good enough for me. You told me you didn't want to be bothered by those no-good, two-faced people at the store.

P_2: George, perhaps it would be better if I heard Esther out before you interrupted. This would enable her to present her picture. Then you could give me your picture without any interruptions from Esther.

G_2: OK. I just find it difficult to listen to these lies she is telling.

E_2: What do you mean, lies? I am telling the truth. You are the liar.

P_3: I am finding it very difficult to find out what either of you perceives the problem to be. You are going to have to stop interrupting and begin

to cooperate. Now Esther, you were saying you
felt neglected. Tell me about your feeling of
being neglected.

In the verbatim above, the communication pattern
between George and Esther was unproductive. Esther
immediately started blaming George for the problem.
Although she was able to pinpoint the problem of George's
work schedule, she presented the problem in such a way
that it provoked George to answer (see E_1). In G_1, George
reacted to Esther's finger-pointing with hostility. This
pattern of communication was preventing the clarification
of the problem.

In P_3, the pastor intervenes actively to point out that their
pattern of communication was preventing clarification of
the problem. In this response, the pastor was taking charge
of the counseling session and was attempting to guide them
into better ways of expressing themselves. He would not let
one spouse interrupt the other. He was teaching them to
respect each other while the other was talking. In this way,
he way laying the foundation for his active teaching role in
their problem-solving. Moreover, the pastor was teaching
the couple, by his intervention, one of the basic essentials of
problem-solving—namely, listening to the other person.

In the following verbatim selection, the method of
cognitive reconstruction will be further illustrated:

P_4: Esther, tell me about your feeling of neglect.
E_3: Well, he would spend so much time at work
that I didn't see him hardly at all. When he
came home, he only had time to eat and sleep.
He didn't have a chance to talk. There were

things that happened during the day which I wanted to talk to him about, but he was not available.

P₅: Sounds like you want to share more of your life with your husband.

E₄: Yes, we used to do a lot of things together. We used to go places. We used to talk a lot. We had some very good times. Now I am missing this with him, because he has that stupid job.

P₆: You really feel like his work has come between a good thing?

E₅: Yes.

P₇: George, your face says you are ready to burst if you don't get a chance to give your side. Let's hear it.

G₆: I never said she was not good enough for me. That's a lie. I have to work those long hours. She doesn't understand the demands.

P₈: You feel misunderstood.

G₇: Yes. I need a wife who supports my efforts to get ahead. But all she does is criticize me for neglecting her.

P₈: Tell me more about your need to be understood.

G₈ Well, I grew up in a family where my mother criticized me a lot. She said I would never amount to very much. I have to show her I am a success. I have to prove something to her.

P₁₀: Sounds like your mother is an important influence in your life.

G₉: Yes. I could never please her. I have never been able to please her. She never liked the way I did things. She didn't like my marriage choice. She says my wife can't raise children, so she had me move in with her so she could watch the children.

P$_{11}$: I am getting a good picture of the problem now. You are spending a lot of time proving something to your mother.

G$_{10}$: Yes.

In P$_4$, the pastor pursued the nature of the problem with Esther. As he focused upon the problem, he learned that Esther's real concern was that things had changed from the way they used to be earlier in the marriage. Her real concern was that she no longer had a sharing relationship with her husband, and she desparately needed and wanted such a relationship with him. George, on the other hand, had a need to be successful in order to please his mother. The purpose of this brief summary is to point out that clarifying the problem helps to focus the problem not only for the pastor, but also for the couple. Through allowing each spouse time to give his or her understanding of the problem, the pastor enabled them to pinpoint the central issues they felt crucial to them. That is to say, there were needs each spouse felt were being neglected by the other spouse. Therefore, in clarifying the events leading up to the crisis, they brought the problem into focus.

GUIDING THE EXPRESSION OF FEELINGS

The pastor was very mindful of the feelings being expressed by each spouse. Through his own experience in marriage, the pastor had become aware that behind marital conflicts are real needs that couples have problems expressing directly. Therefore, he attempted to guide each spouse to express his or her real feelings.

The pastor attempted to use the method of putting into words what he perceived each person was actually feeling. This method is evident in P_5, P_6, P_8, and P_{10}. In this way, the pastor was teaching the couple that their concerns were real and that he respected and accepted their concerns as real. Moreover, he was helping the couple to see another side of their problem which they had not seen. This method also helps each person focus upon his or her own needs, rather than on the spouse's inadequate response to that need. In reality, he was teaching each partner that behind the complaint of the other were real concerns and that each of them needed to pay more attention to the hidden message in the other's words.

By helping each spouse to express his or her true feelings, the pastor served as a role model for the couple. They learned from the pastor to look behind the words for the real feelings of the other. They learned from the counselor ways to enable each other to be more open to his or her feelings.

In summary, the pastor guided the expression of feelings through expressing what he felt each spouse was saying. He also served as an example of what he hoped they would learn about listening to each other's feelings.

TASK ORIENTATION

Focusing on feelings remains very important throughout the marital intervention. The pastor must always be sensitive to the feelings of all those involved. However, he or she needs to move actively beyond the feelings to the family boundaries. Feelings are essential in providing focus in the beginning, because they help facilitate communication between the family and the pastor. In the case of the Jones family, for example, the pastor needed to go beyond the feelings so that he could help the family improve their subsystem boundaries.

In the analysis of the Jones family in the last chapter, it was pointed out that the boundaries between the subsystems were blurred. Therefore, the pastor decided to involve the whole family—the spouses, the children, and the mother-in-law—because of the need to strengthen the family boundaries. Consequently he asked the couple to bring in the children and the mother-in-law. This was done after the pastor had had two interviews with the couple and had visited the home of the family. The home visits were used to help the pastor diagnose the family dynamics. Below is a portion of a verbatim report of the first interview with the whole family:

> P_1: I guess you are wondering why I called the whole family together. As you know, I have been seeing your mother and father and your son and daughter-in-law together. *(He was addressing the children and mother/mother-in-law.)* In talking with them, I have gotten some idea of where their hurt is. Could you give me some idea where you think the family hurt is?

> ML_1: I think the problem is the children. I mean that George and Esther are too lenient with the children. The children need more discipline, and I am glad I am around to give it to them.

> P_2: So, Mrs. Jones, you see the problem as lack of

discipline of the children . . .

ML₂: Yes, and I . . .

P₃: Well, children, you have a chance to say where you feel the pain is in the family. Please speak up, because your opinions are so necessary. *(The other children look to the oldest sister to speak.)*

C₃: You see, mom and dad need to do more things together. They just don't do things the way they use to.

P₄: How do you feel about this?

C₄: You see, I would be much relieved if I could feel they were doing things together again.

C₄: You would feel more comfortable?

C₅: Yes. I think so. It makes me feel very nervous when things are the way they are now.

P₆: How do the rest of you feel? *(Speaking to the other children, who nod their heads in agreement.)*

P₇: Let us assume that the problem in the family is the fact that mommy and daddy need to do more things together. How could you help them do this?

ML₇: That's not the problem. They are neglecting the children already. They don't need to spend more time with each other. They need to spend more time with the children.

P₈: Mrs. Jones (ML), I see you have a particular view of the problem. But I want to ask you how could you help your son and daughter-in-law be together more than they currently are?

ML$_8$: I am not sure I understand what you mean.

P$_9$: For example, let us role-play a scene where George comes home tired after a long day's work. Children, do what you generally do when dad comes home. Mrs. Jones, could you do what you normally do? Esther and George, try to follow your normal pattern. The goal is to recreate as closely as you can the actual way things are at home when dad comes home.

> *The Role Play: Mr. Jones came into the room. He acted as though he was going straight to the kitchen to eat. The children were role-playing a fighting scene. They almost ignored the fact that their father had come home. While the mother tried to talk with her husband, the children would interrupt her with complaints about each other. During all of this, the mother-in-law entered the room and began to complain to George about the children's behavior during the day.*

After the role play, the pastor asked them to role-play a different scene. However, this time he directed the children to greet their father rather than to ignore him. Then the pastor told them to find something creative to do while their mother prepared the meal. He also told them not to run to their mother with their problems, but to try to solve them by themselves. He instructed the mother-in-law to sit quietly without bothering the couple or the children. He also told George and Esther to try to share their day while she was preparing the meal.

In the next role play, the children found it hard to keep out of their parent's way. Moreover, the mother-in-law continued to intrude, and George and Esther could not find much to discuss. When the children or mother-in-law intruded into the spouses' conversation, the pastor would remind them that they were interfering. At one point, he left the couple alone to join the children in order to help them find something creative to do.[1] Before leaving the couple alone, he instructed them to attempt a communications exercise.[2]

In further sessions, the pastor had the family continue the role-playing of scenes of the actual situation at home. He also got the family to continue to experiment with new ways of relating at home that would help the spouse subsystem to function. After about six visits, the family was actively trying to protect their spouse subsystem. However, more work needed to help the mother-in-law find a creative way to relate to the family.

Comment: When the pastor brought the whole family together, he moved as quickly as he could to the task of helping the spouse subsystem to function adequately. In P_7, the pastor began to ask questions concerning how the children could help strengthen the spouse subsystem.

Task orientation is important for several reasons. First, it gives the family a sense that it is working on the problem in a concrete way. Many black families need an immediate success so that they can have hope of overcoming the family problem. The task-oriented problem-solving method of family therapy offers this opportunity.

Second, children often find it hard to sit still during many of the verbal exchanges in the interviews. Therefore, it is important to get the children to participate in the solving of the family problem as soon as they can. The role playing and the reenactment of family problems are very crucial as a method of mobilizing children's energy.

Third, the black pastor is part of a tradition in which he or she is expected to be an active leader. Black pastors find it hard to sit back and be passive in their counseling. The active task orientation of problem-solving allows them to utilize their aggressive gifts in a constructive way to help the family grow.

Several methods were used in helping the Jones family focus upon its problem. The first was reenacting the family problem. In P_9, the pastor asked the family to reconstruct a normal scene that would take place in the family. Reenactment of the family problem gave the Joneses an opportunity to see themselves in action as well as showing the pastor where he needed to intervene. Also, in having them recreate a typical family scene, the pastor enabled all the family members to be involved in an active way.

The second method used was intended to help the family develop different patterns of relating. Once the family role-played the typical way in which they solved problems, the pastor sought to change this pattern by helping the family members experiment with different patterns of relating. For example, he asked the mother-in-law not to intervene. He asked the children to find more creative ways to play. He also asked George and Esther to share their lives with each other more. In this way the pastor was trying to enable them to rehearse, in his presence and under his leadership, new ways of relating. By such methods, the pastor hoped to help the family develop new boundaries between their subsystems.

It must also be added here that the role-playing of actual problems, and experimenting with new patterns of relating, can be continued session after session until the crisis is over. Moreover, the spouse subsystem does not have to be the focus; any subsystem or relationship within the family can be the focus, depending upon the pastor's diagnosis and the family's presenting problem. For example, if the father does not have an adequate relationship with the children, and if this seems to be the focal point of the family's problem, the pastor would need to concentrate on helping the father to relate to them. The pastor has many alternatives for intervention in families when boundary theory is used.

In summarizing this section, it must be emphasized that counseling involving task orientation and the reenactment of actual family problems has a lot to contribute to black families. First, role reenactment is suitable for families that are not future-oriented; that is, it is relevant to families that need immediate successes and cannot wait many long months for the results. Second, this task-oriented approach is good for those families that have not learned the language of psychology and thus would not be able to profit from long-term, insight-oriented therapy. Third, short-term counseling is convenient for the minister who has limited time because of the many demands of the church. This short-term, task-oriented approach to family therapy, then, is a natural model for the needs of many black families and for the needs of many black pastors.

CONCLUSION

The crisis in the Jones family represented an opportunity for intervention by the black pastor to guide healthy crisis-coping within the family. In guiding the Jones family, the pastor combined the active teaching approach of black pastoral care with the methods and theories of family boundary therapy. This wedding of tradition and theory illustrates how it is possible for the black church to continue its traditional role of strengthening black families.

CONCLUSION

In conclusion, let us review the basic argument of the book along with a few comparisons between black pastoral care and modern pastoral care. Also we shall see the relevance of modern pastoral care.

I have attempted in this book to examine pastoral care in the black church. My basic argument is that sustaining and guiding became the dominant forms of pastoral care in the black church because of historical-cultural circumstances that existed in America. I have also maintained that economic and political realities have prevented healing from becoming a dominant goal in black pastoral care. These factors have formed the background that distinguishes black pastoral care from modern pastoral care, which has emphasized healing because its practitioners have possessed the economic resources and educational opportunities to obtain the training necessary to pursue healing as a goal.

There are other comparisons that can be made between black pastoral care and modern pastoral care as it exists in white churches. Much discussion exists in the field of pastoral care concerning the relevance of the Christian tradition in caring for persons. Some writers are criticizing the church because its healing model has been based upon the secular behavioral science models rather than upon the richness of the Christian tradition. In contrast, black pastoral care has emerged out of a rich Christian tradition rooted in theology. Black pastoral care has been rooted in a faith in an incarnate God who has been active in the lives of the oppressed. It has utilized the ritualistic ceremonies and the communal worship of the church to carry out its ministry. The actual caring has taken place in a communal setting where the pastor has been a symbol presiding over the caring community. It has been through this caring community that God has sought to bring liberation to black Christians.

Modern pastoral care has also been critized for utilizing nondirective techniques at the expense of the moral guiding functions inherent in Christian tradition. This criticism is clearly the approach of Don S. Browning's work, the *Moral Context of Pastoral Care.*[1] Although the counseling task of the black pastor does not specifically emphasize discipline and

socialization, as Brown does, it does highlight the significance of the role of the black pastor as custodian of the
symbolic universe of the black Christian. Black Christians
have looked to the black pastor as the one who could help
them find meaning in a hostile world and who could help
guide them through the dark valleys and shadows caused
by oppression. He or she has also been expected to provide
leadership and give direction to the confused lives of
persons whose earthly power has been frustrated. It can be
concluded that black pastoral care has not ignored the value
of guiding in favor of the symbolic role of the black pastor.

Although there are several contrasts between black
pastoral care and modern pastoral care, this does not mean
that the discoveries in modern pastoral care are irrelevant to
the black church. The contributions of modern pastoral care
will become increasingly valuable as the black laity becomes
better educated and assumes greater leadership in the
wider society in the future. The church will not be able to
exert a controlling influence over people's lives. Because of
this decreasing influence, the enabling ministries of modern
pastoral care may have relevance to black pastoral care. The
significance of modern pastoral care is that it helps develop
a person's inner resources. In the future, the black pastor
will have to use his or her symbolic role to release the innate
potentials of black people. The pastor's parenting and
directing will need to be done with the goal of releasing
people's God-given talent for self-direction. Black people
have been children too long; and the black pastor, as
symbolic leader and custodian of their world view, will
need to help them leave Egypt without looking back
wishing to reenter slavery.

NOTES

Chapter I

1. William A. Clebsch and Charles R. Jaekle, *Pastoral Care in Historical Perspective* (Englewood, N.J.: Prentice-Hall, 1964), pp. 8-10.

2. Joseph Washington, *Black Sects and Cults* (Garden City, N.Y.: Doubleday, 1972). He introduces the concept of black religion's purpose of gaining power or uniting with sources of power in the world.

3. See Edward E. Thornton, *Professional Education for Ministry* (Nashville: Abingdon, 1970), pp. 31-33. See also William Hulme, *Pastoral Care Come of Age* (Abingdon, 1970). These works show the influence of the one-to-one medical model orientation and the beginnings of a movement away from this orientation in pastoral care.

4. E. Franklin Frazier, *The Negro Church in America* (New York: Schocken

Books, 1964), p. 16. He examines the black church as an invisible institution during early slavery.

5. E. Mansell Pattison, *Pastor and Parish: A System Approach* (Philadelphia: Fortress Press, 1977), p. 34. This work provides a helpful examination of the function of the community symbol.

6. Frazier, *The Negro Church,* p. 33.

7. *Ibid.,* p. 34.

8. *Ibid.,* p. 35.

9. *Ibid.*

10. Melville J. Herskovits, *The New World Negro* (Bloomington: The University of Indiana Press, 1966), p. 141.

11. Benjamin E. Mays and Joseph W. Nicholson, *The Negro's Church* (New York: Institute of Social and Religious Research, 1933; reprinted, New York: Arno Press, 1969), p. 14.

12. *Ibid.,* p. 110.

13. Vattell E. Daniel, "Ritual and Stratification in Chicago Negro Churches," *American Sociological Review,* June, 1942, pp. 360-61.

14. Pattison, *Pastor and Parish,* p. 63

15. This is the conclusion made by Charles V. Hamilton, *The Black Preacher in America* (New York: Morrow, 1972), pp. 14-15.

16. Floyd Massey, Jr., and Samuel B. McKinney, *Church Administration in the Black Perspective* (Valley Forge, Pa.: Judson Press, 1976), pp. 34-35.

Chapter II

1. Floyd Massey, Jr., and Samuel B. McKinney, *Church Administration in the Black Perspective* (Valley Forge, Pa.: Judson Press, 1976), p. 34.

2. William A. Clebsch and Charles R. Jaekle, *Pastoral Care in Historical Perspective* (Englewood, N.J.: Prentice-Hall, 1964), p. 44.

3. *Ibid.,* p. 47.

4. *Ibid.,* p. 48.

Chapter IV

1. Howard Thurman, *The Negro Spiritual Speaks to Life and Death* (New York: Harper, 1947), pp. 13-14.

2. Melvile J. Herskovits, *The Myth of the Negro Past* (Gloucester, Mass.: Peter Smith, 1970), p. 198.

3. For a contemporary examination of modern funeral practices, see Morris J. McDonald, "The Management of Grief: A Study of Black Funeral Practices," *Omega,* Summer, 1973, pp. 139-48.

4. Herskovits, *Myth of the Negro Past,* p. 202.

5. *Ibid.,* p. 203.

6. Maurice Jackson, "The Black Experience With Death: A Brief Analysis Through Black Writings," *Omega* (August, 1972, p. 204. In this article Jackson compares the black experience of death with that of other ethnic groups.

Chapter V

1. William A. Clebsch and Charles R. Jaekle, *Pastoral Care in Historical Perspective* (Englewood, N.J.: Prentice-Hall, 196), p. 50.

2. See Genesis 2:24, Ephesians 5:31 for the biblical passage concerning the relationship of spouses to parents.

3. This insight reflects a conversation with Grant S. Shockley, President of the Interdenominational Theological Center.

Chapter VI

1. Comments made to me on June 5, 1977, during the preparation of this book.

2. In *Church Administration in the Black Perspective,* pp. 46-47. Floyd Massey and Samuel B. McKinney point out that many persons in the Bapist denomination prefer formally trained pastors. This preference reflects the laity's awareness of the needs of young people.

3. These terms and their usage came from Homer L. Jernigan's lecture of October 26, 1973, at Boston University School of Theology.

4. For details of adoption practices in the black community see Melville J. Herkovits, *The Myth of the Negro Past* (Gloucester, Mass.: Peter Smith, 1970), pp. 187-88.

5. For a discussion of the extended family in Africa, see John S. Mbiti, *African Religions and Philosophy* Garden City, N.Y.: Doubleday, 1970), p. 139.

6. Grant S. Shockley concludes that black churches have never reached more than a minority of black youth. For more details, read his "Christian Education and the Black Church: A Contextual Approach," *The Journal of the Interdenominational Theological Center,* Spring, 1975, p. 85.

7. See chapter 1 for details relative to the role of the black church in black families.

8. Herskovits, *The Myth of the Negro Past,* p. 199.

9. *Ibid.,* p. 150.

10. *Ibid.*

11. *Ibid.,* p. 152.

12. Thomas J. Pugh and Emily H. Mudd, "Attitudes of Black Women and Men Toward Using Community Services," *Journal of Religion and Health,* July, 1971, pp. 272-274.

Chapter VII

1. Deotis Roberts, *Liberation and Reconciliation,* (Philadelphia: Westminster Press), pp. 60-61.

2. For a good explanation of boundary theory, see Salvador Minuchin, *et al., Families of the Slums: An Exploration of Their Structure and Treatment* (New York: Basic Books, 1967).

3. See Salvador Minuchin, *Families and Family Therapy* (Cambridge: Harvard University Press, 1974), pp. 56-69, for details on the functions of subsystems in families.

Chapter VIII

1. What the pastor did was to explore with them how it felt to be alone without their mother stopping them from fighting. Then he began to show them ways to settle arguments by setting up a council of elders. The children not in the dispute became mediating elders for the disputing children.

2. Many communication exercises could be attempted. Virginia Satir has outlined many games for couples in her publication *Peoplemaking* (Palo Alto: Science and Behavior Books), pp. 80-96. For example, Esther is a finger pointer or a blamer. She always says, "You did this or that to me." The pastor instructed Esther to say what she really meant by substituting *"I need* for *you. . . . "* An example would be, "George, I need you to be with me more often."

Conclusion

1. Don S. Browning, *The Moral Context of Pastoral Care* (Philadelphia: Westminster Press, 1976).